Vernon Noble

NICKNAMES

Past and Present

Foreword by Eric Partridge

Hamish Hamilton
LONDON

First published in Great Britain 1976
by Hamish Hamilton Ltd
90 Great Russell Street London WC1B 3PT

Copyright © 1976 by Vernon Noble

SBN 241 89514 6

Printed in Great Britain by
Western Printing Services Ltd, Bristol

For Jean who shared my love of words;
and for Andrew and Nicholas
who I hope will do so

Contents

Foreword

A nickname is not, as some would-be wit has suggested, a name bestowed in the nick of time, but an additional name, an 'also' name, an *eke-name*; late middle English *nekename*. To the sense 'additional' we have to subjoin the derivative, 'substituted', especially if bestowed in ridicule or irony. Clearly, the ridicule changes sometimes to affection, or even to admiration, as when hitherto disregarded or despised 'local boy makes good'.

The nicknames in Vernon Noble's book are historical ones, including those of sport. He also includes what he describes as 'package' words, or short verbless groups of words, which he neatly calls 'nicknames' close relatives'. Such words, he suggests, signify much in little and have been accepted into the language. Most such words have historical importance or, at least, historical aptness, often allied to wit.

What I like most in the always interesting Introduction is the section 'Omissions'. The author thereby forestalls not only those reviewers who, usually without thinking, ask why this or that, or the other class or kind of words or word-groups, has not been treated, but also those readers who—needless to say—have not read the Introduction (and have thus deprived themselves of a lively pleasure) 'stick their necks out' and write indignantly. Such letters to the author might ask, 'Why haven't you told us why, when a man surnamed Rhodes or Rhoades is inevitably nicknamed "Dusty", that appellation is bestowed also on every Miller, or why, if a very tall man becomes "Lofty", a big, brawny fellow becomes "Tiny"; or why a red-haired man becomes "Bluey".' Then there's the ex-soldier or it may be a seaman, or a former airman, who 'wants to know' why his regiment's or battleship's or aircraft-type's nickname isn't there.

For the same good reason (see the Introduction, please) the

author excludes nicknames for 'nationals'—counties and cities —trades and professions—plants—mammals—football teams— and so forth. Mostly he excludes slang and, in so doing, has some notable things to say. He explains all these exclusions and others in the general statement he rightly makes, that he wished to present an entity; a justifiable, very proper, subject for a book; a convenience and an entertainment.

The conclusion truly concludes, but in so doing it also provides the reviewer with welcome gist, the scholar with food for chewing, and—far, far more important—the reader with enduring entertainment and solid information attractively foreshadowed. It's obvious, yet, for some, a necessary intimation; that Mr Noble is very well read indeed, and he knows how to apply what he has so widely gleaned.

I don't intend to pick out plums from an imaginary many-climed orchard, for the reader would need too many baskets. On the other hand, I wish to emphasise a feature of composition, a style of writing, so generally taken for granted that one becomes conscious of it only when it is lacking: a quality possessed by comparatively few writers and disconcertingly few journalists; the latter do, however, attain, other things being unequal, a higher proportion of competency. And that is the quality of sheer professionalism, which, naturally enough, tends to be acquired in the highest degree by journalists-become-authors and by writers not inexperienced in the arts and needs of journalism.

Vernon Noble is not merely a shining but also a salutary example of former journalist and present author. He is a real professional, an examplar of an acquired virtue, the virtue you see in such novelists as Stanley Weyman and A. E. W. Mason and in such contemporary novelists as H. E. Bates and—well, I think not. 'No names, no pack-drill.' You see it also in such historians as Trevelyan and (Sir) William Keith Hancock; in such philosophers as Collingwood; in such playwrights as Coward and (Sir Terence) Rattigan and John Mortimer. To name all the characteristics of this not too common gift would be tedious. Yet one can hardly, in either decency or common sense, fail to mention conscientiousness and accuracy; fairness of attitude; a style commensurate with the subject; freedom from self-conceit and pretentiousness. With few exceptions, you will not find these professionals, except in the way of duty or other need, at cocktail parties and such other button-holing, self-seeking and self-promoting, affairs frequented by those who come, both to gaze and to be gazed at or, at worst, be seen. The genuine professional does not go in order to be seen, merely to see and to note what he has observed; a remark as applicable to travel-writers and novelists as to journalists.

Vernon Noble is a born observer, whether of people and events or in his reading. A richly experienced journalist,then, after World War Two, a B.B.C. man, yet always, both potentially and in the fact, a writer.

I first met him when, that 'lowest form of human life', an AC2, I joined 'the writers' team' at the Air Ministry early in 1945. In addition to Alan Walbank, Ronnie Delderfield, and our esteemed Wing Commander Dudley Barker, himself a journalist and an author, I found that the section housed the RAF's Official Observers, John Pudney, H. E. Bates, Vernon Noble and John Bentley. The first three were Squadron Leaders, Bentley a Flight Lieutenant; I was a supernumerary, acting partly as a corrective and partly in writing articles, my proudest achievement being three for the Russian department of information—proud because they highly commended my efforts. All those officers were exceedingly nice to me; especially John Pudney and Vernon Noble. The Observers went, not unnaturally, on missions abroad, as did several of the flight lieutenants.

Once, while Vernon happened to be in the building, he did me a particularly good, yet entirely characteristic, turn. Back from lunch, I heard a telephone ringing at Squadron Leader (now Sir) Geoffrey Harmsworth's desk (he was the internal 'Admin' officer), so I answered it. A very abrupt voice asked whether AC2 Partridge were there. 'Yes—*speaking!*' 'Well, look, AC2'—most disagreeable stress on '2'—'Partridge, why haven't you been doing guard and picket duties? You may be attached to Air Ministry, but for discipline, you come under Headquarters Unit.'—'Because, *sir*, I hold a medical certificate exempting me from all fatigues and guards, *et cetera*.' 'I don't think that's good enough, Partridge. We're rather short-handed.' At this point, Vernon who had noticed that I seemed to be in trouble, joined me and, with a 'May I?' gesture, took the receiver and said 'Who is that speaking?'—'Warrant Officer X.'—'Yes, and what, precisely, do you want *Mr*

Partridge for?' After a pause, 'Right! Well, this is Squadron Leader Noble speaking. You haven't a leg to stand on—Partridge is fully excused from outside duties, and even if he weren't, we would soon see to it that he should be. To *you*, he may be just another 'body'; to us, he's invaluable. Have you *got* that? Good! And I warn you, Warrant Officer, that if I hear of you again interfering in this utterly unnecessary and time-wasting manner, I'll ensure that disciplinary measures be taken against you. What's more, this is a final warning.' I thanked Vernon. His only reply was, 'Least I could do. These petty Hitlers!'

In PR3 (Public Relations Section Three) I came, during the five or six months up to my being appositely discharged on Independence Day, to know the staff pretty well. Whereas three of them consistently exhibited a certain *panache*, Vernon went about his work quietly and efficiently, for he and our 'Wingco' were first-class journalists: in short, true professionals.

Vernon Noble, however, has always been far more than that. Without effusiveness—I can visualise him shuddering at the thought—and without display, he possesses profound sentiment without a grain of sentimentality; businesslike without fuss and without hardness; one who would blush to have his kindness and generosities publicised—or mentioned to a group— or, person to person, gratefully acknowledged.

Perhaps what I am trying to convey is the fact that, whether in his everyday life or in his writings, he radiates a not always immediately detectable, yet a pervasive, and invariable, warmth of character. To say more about his personality would embarrass him. About his books, I can—and I must—state that no one of any sense or sensitiveness or sensibility could fail to perceive, and to appreciate, the warmth that comes in a benign, and beneficient, undazzling, grateful glow from *Girls, You Amaze Me*, (about the Women's Auxiliary Air Force), 1943—manifestly one of his Air Ministry publications and based on his experiences on bomber stations; *The Man in Leather Breeches*, published ten years later, with the sub-title, 'The Life and Times of George Fox'; his other biographies, including one of William Penn; and his charming, delightful, *un*condescending books for children.

Those few pieces of information will rightly have led you to suppose that Vernon Noble has written—for he has *written*, not merely compiled—this book, not for academics (although they could learn a thing or two or three about the presentation of well-researched material alchemied into an admirable read-ability) but for that best of all reading publics: the general intelligent, the normally educated, public.

Here you have a dictionary, informal and trustworthy that will leave a pleasant taste on the palate. I'd be proud to have written it: I *am* proud to be accounted the author's friend.

ERIC PARTRIDGE

March 1976

Abbreviations and Acknowledgments

c   about the year
cf.   compare
q.v.   which see
DSUE Eric Partridge, *A Dictionary of Slang and Unconventional English*, London, Routledge and Kegan Paul, 1970
ODEE *The Oxford Dictionary of English Etymology* (Ed. C. T. Onions), Oxford, Clarendon Press, 1969
SOED *The Shorter Oxford English Dictionary*, Oxford, Clarendon Press, 1972

Biblical quotations are from *Common Bible* (Ecumenical Edition), London, Collins, 1973

I have consulted *The Concise Dictionary of National Biography*, Oxford, University Press, 1969

See note on etymology at the end of the Introduction.

I wish to express my gratitude to my friend Eric Partridge for his encouragement and advice; and to that journalistic expert on astronomical affairs, Patrick Moore, for his kindness in supplying me with a definition of 'black hole'.

I am also beholden to the librarian and staff at Marple library in Cheshire for their efficiency and courtesy.

Introduction

When I was a boy and first became enthralled by the wonder of words (in a school, by the way, where Latin was taught as an exciting language) there was a clash of opinion between the English master and the History master. The former frowned on nicknames: the latter revelled in them. My allegiance in this respect was to the History master, although my affection for his colleague is undimmed after more than half a century because of the wide range of literature to which he introduced us.

The English text book was William Murison's *English Composition*, Cambridge, University Press, a perfect guide to the niceties of language. We were advised that 'Great attention should be paid to the exact meanings of words. Much help comes from reading widely in classic authors, old as well as new—we must know the old usage as distinct from the new; from continual reference to some standard dictionary; and from listening to good speakers both in private and in public.' Was there ever better advice to a boy at the outset of his adventure into the world of communication, or to the aspiring writer!

Mr Murison, however, was rather cramping to the compiler of a dictionary such as this one I have attempted. He warned against what he called 'barbarisms', and among these he included 'archaic, obsolete words; dialectic, provincial words; slang; technical terms; foreign words; neologisms'. Nevertheless, he admitted that there might be occasions when a word from any of these classes was admissible, but one had to be extremely careful. The slang he most abhorred was not 'beak' for magistrate or headmaster, and suchlike vulgarisms, but 'the indiscriminate use of *awful, awfully, nice* . . .'. That was the kind of man Mr Murison was.

He did not condescend even to a paragraph on nicknames, and in a list of foreign words which he said were 'as a rule, inexcusable' he included *soubriquet*. He was all for plain, forth-right English and foreign imports were to be countenanced only if they expressed some meaning for which our own vocabulary was inadequate, never for showing-off. He did allow, in his long list of figures of speech, the use of a name to denote a characteristic—antonomasia—such as Solomon for a wise man, and Croesus for a rich one.

With such a mentor it was understandable that our English master regarded nicknames as too closely related to slang to be encouraged, and it was typical of him that on one occasion when a boy used the word 'bowler' in an essay, he commented: 'If you mean bowler hat, why not say so?' And whenever he heard a reference to a 'bobby' his face took on a painful expression. And Americanisms seemed to give him indigestion.

The History master, on the other hand, explained how 'bobby' began to tread the linguistic beat, and set us wondering why it had outlived 'peeler'; why king John was called 'lack-land' and whether his brother deserved the title 'lion heart'. We sometimes put aside the period of history we were supposed to be studying and went off into by-ways that would have shocked a school inspector. Once you are on the track of a nickname the dates are of no particular significance: you stalk the word until you have captured and subdued it and dissected it. Then, after such an excursion, the master would bring us back to the point of departure, knowing that he had whetted our appetite and that we would search for more—or, at least, some of us would. That is how good teachers are made.

Nicknames personalise history. They bring the king, the statesman, the warrior to life. What schoolboy would not want to know more about those valiant Vikings, Eric Bloodaxe, Harald Bluetooth and Ivar the Boneless? The Vikings were fond of nicknames and some of these are commemorated in place names. C. Stella Davies and John Levitt give examples in *What's in a Name*, London, Routledge and Kegan Paul, 1970. One of these is Scarborough, the fortified village of Thorgils Skaroi, the Scandinavian personal name being tacked on to the Anglo-Saxon 'borough' or 'burg', a fortified place. Skaroi was a nickname meaning 'hare-lip'. From

2

William 'the conqueror' to Edward 'the peacemaker'—and all the other Edwards such as 'the martyr' and 'the confessor'; from Harold 'harefoot' to Dizzy and the widow at Windsor, there was a long gallery of portraits to be surveyed, introducing us to real people—as real as 'fatso' at the next desk, or 'four-eyes' who wore glasses, or 'whiskers' who taught us chemistry and mumbled through a hanging white moustache.

It was salutary to be warned not to take honorifics at their face value, a kind of instant history in which one monarch was labelled 'the good' and another 'the great'; one 'the bad' and another 'the wise'. It was a lesson in discrimination, in inquiry as to whether a monarch merited the description he was saddled with, complimentary or otherwise; a lesson, too, in charity, because nobody is entirely good or entirely bad.

I have excluded most honorifics from this dictionary. There are too many of them—too many 'greats' such as Alfred, Frederick and Alexander; too many 'goods', from 'good queen Bess' for Elizabeth I to Victoria who inherited the appellation after the death of her consort, 'Albert the good'. There is a massive magnificat of such terms in European history, a paean of praise from grateful or sycophantic subjects, an admiring simplification of attributes beloved of the writers of old school books. The Charleses seem to have been especially honoured. To take just a few examples:

Charles 'the good' (c1084–1127), count of Flanders, also called Charles 'the Dane' because he was the only son of Canute IV, king of Denmark; Charles 'the bold' (1433–77), duke of Burgundy, son of Philip 'the good'; Charles V (1337–80), king of France, known as 'the wise'; Charles III (1361–1425), king of Navarre, called 'the noble', son of Charles II, 'the bad'; and Charles II (1661–1700), king of Spain, known as 'the desired'. The list is a long one.

Nicknames were by no means always straightforwardly 'good' or 'bad'—and even the bad ones had a certain relish, like that of Robert I, duke of Normandy, who died in 1035, surnamed 'the devil' and about whom there are many legends—but might refer to some characteristic, physical or otherwise. Charles III (879–929), king of France, was called 'the simple': he was the son of Louis 'the stammerer'. Charles III (832–88), Roman emperor and king of the West Franks became known as 'the fat'. I wonder what his predecessor, Charles II (son of

Louis 'the pious') thought of his nickname '*le chauve*'—bald-headed, 'Which Karlé Calvus cleped was', as Gower puts it in his *Confessio Amantis*. In the years when there seemed to be a lack of imagination in the choice of Christian names, and royal parents on the continent could not get much further than Charles and Louis, a nickname of some kind was useful.

Then we have another kind of honorific, bestowed on commoners who have achieved distinction, posthumously awarded, far too numerous to be included here. There are too many 'fathers'—Roger Ascham, 'father of English prose'; Thomas Tallis, 'father of English music'; Henry Fielding, 'father of the English novel'; and, further afield and deeper into the past, Herodotus, 'father of history'; Hippocrates, 'father of medicine': and even Satan, 'father of lies'. The list goes on and on, commemorating the pioneers—William Caxton, 'father of English printing'; Isaac Walton, 'father of angling'; and Thomas Tompion, 'father of English clockmaking'. And on the political side, such people as Eamon de Valera, 'father of the Irish Republic' (also known as 'the chief'), statesman, military leader and president who died in 1975 at the age of ninety-two. Let us leave them to their glory.

Thomas Aquinas, 'the angelic doctor' is matched by our own Roger Bacon, 'the wonderful doctor', and by 'moral Gower', as Chaucer in *Troilus and Cressida* called his friend. And we have 'rare' Ben Jonson, and Thomas Carlyle, 'the sage of Chelsea' because he lived there; and across the Channel, 'the divine Sarah' (Bernhardt); and, of course, 'bluff king Hal', Henry VIII. ('Bluff' originally meant 'broad-faced'.)

Nicknames such as these, and the more ingenious and interesting listed in this dictionary, enrich and enliven the language. They are the products of men's wits and show the desire for descriptive labels of identification. What's in a name? A man's whole lifetime summarised, perhaps, or merely some quirk or characteristic that marked him out among his fellows, or his part in some passing episode. Personal nicknames can be earned, deserved or thrust upon one with malic aforethought: others sometimes come about by the company one keeps.

Not only has each name a place in history, a niche in the story of its particular period, but the word itself often has a distinguished ancestry, and this I have tried to trace. Etymology goes hand-in-hand with social change and development. Some

4

words go back to a long-forgotten past; some change their meaning, subtly or violently; some are lost for ever and new ones take their place. Some linger only in dialect, the repository of so much of our linguistic history—not only the words themselves but the way they are pronounced—the living relics of our invaders whose language as well as themselves we absorbed.

Declaration of Intent

This is a dictionary of British nicknames for people (following Mr Murison's advice I will not use 'soubriquet', or 'sobriquet', anglicized though it may have become), things and events, and a few from foreign fields—especially from America—which we have adopted. The dictionary also includes what may be described as 'package' words because they are nicknames' close relatives and have been accepted into the language, signifying much in little: Cliveden set, middle ages, the reformation, the renaissance are obvious examples. With each word or groups of words is a potted history or explanation, a derivation of a word itself where appropriate, with quotations to illustrate usage in many cases.

The dictionary definition of 'nickname'—that it is a name additional to a proper name or substituted for it, usually in ridicule or pleasantry—needs now, I suggest, to be enlarged, with more stress on the *eke* of the middle English *ekename* (corrupted to *nekename*), because of its derivation from the first English *ecan*, to increase. (We still have the original meaning in such an expression as 'to eke out the family budget'. As far back as John Lydgate (c1370–1451) it is used in this way when in one of his poems he writes: 'Or more their bounty for to eke'.) So that the dictionary definition of a name given in addition to the proper one could well be extended to the 'package' word that I mentioned. Words grow: language is a living, changing thing: even the latest dictionary cannot keep pace with some of the nuances of meaning.

Incidentally, Shakespeare seems to use 'nickname' as a verb of ridicule, when in *Love's Labour's Lost* (V. ii) the king says, 'The virtue of your eye must break my oath', and the princess replies, 'You nickname virtue; vice you should have spoke.'

In the following lists I have included familiar nicknames and terms that one comes across in literature and history, and others which have dropped by the wayside but which seem to be worthy of recall, reminding us of personalities, sects and groups that our forefathers knew. As well as looking to the past I have tried to foresee what names and words familiar in the journalism, broadcasting and literature of the time at which I write will be of interest in the future.

The aim is to interest, inform and entertain, and in the hope that there will be some stimulation to further inquiry into the personalities and incidents referred to.

There has had to be drastic pruning in a time-span from biblical days to the latter half of the twentieth century. No dictionary of this kind can even approach the definitive, and to be of any value it must restrict its scope. That is why it is necessary to discuss deliberate omissions, lest a reader waste his time searching for what is not there. Most of the categories omitted are comprehensively dealt with by other dictionaries devoted to the particular subject.

Omissions

In addition to honorifics already referred to, a notable omission is that of the familiar form of a Christian (or first) name, such as Bill for William, Jim for James, Dick for Richard, Bob or Robin for Robert, Bess and Betty for Elizabeth, and so on. Most of them, I would have thought, are too well-known to be worth recording, and need little explanation. They are accepted diminutives. Some have their attractions and little histories. Why, for example, should a former British prime minister, Edward (Richard George) Heath, always be known as Ted, and Edward VII be nicknamed Teddy when his family called him Bertie? Edward is one of the oldest of English Christian names, and people have played about with the letters in it, producing Ned and Ted for no particular reason. Unless, of course, it originated in baby-talk, as many of these diminutives do. Ed leads to Ned and Ted, and they are easier to say than Edward. Compare nanny for granny, the 'gr' being difficult for a child to get its tongue around; and Nol for Oliver.

And how did Margaret become Peg, as in the case of Mrs Margaret Thatcher who succeeded Mr Heath as leader of the Conservative party in 1975 and was referred to in some journals as Peggy Thatcher? Margaret is also a name of ancient origin, and in Britain has suffered from much juggling of abbreviations and diminutives—Mog, Margo, Madge, Magge, Maggie, Megge, Meg—and Peg to rhyme with the last one, and with its variations of Peggy.

Then there are the pet names for famous people, used in the intimacy of the family or by friends. This is a class on its own. Most families have their nicknames for sons and daughters—and often for their dogs and cats—as if the diminutive were not enough: holy terror, suck-a-thumb, dirty Dick, miss head-in-air, fancy pants; all affectionately descriptive and meeting a need for domestic fun. School nicknames persist among friends into adult life, often embarrassingly so. 'Cave' was the unkind nickname which school chums bestowed on Charles Kingsley because of his large mouth, often opened when he tried to overcome his stutter. (See Susan Chitty, *The Beast and the Monk*, London, Hodder and Stoughton, 1975.) P. G. Wodehouse was known as 'Plum' to his family and friends, and Janet Hitchman tells us in her biography of Dorothy L. Sayers, *Such a Strange Lady*, London, New English Library, 1975, that the versatile novelist and creator of Lord Peter Wimsey was known as 'Swanny' in her younger days because of her long neck. Sir Harold Wilson, Labour prime minister, was nicknamed 'Willie' at his council school, (and 'Houdini of politics' in later life).

The young princess Victoria who was to become queen was called Drina by her family, the shortening of Alexandrina, one of her Christian names in honour of one of her godfathers, tsar Alexander of Russia. Dr Johnson gave the pet name of Tetty to his beloved wife Elizabeth, much older than himself and who died in 1752 after only fifteen years of marriage. Topsy was the name that Godon Craig gave to Isadora Duncan during their passionate love affair with its long exchange of letters.

Among the companions of the prince of Wales who was to become George IV were members of the Barrymore family, each with a whimsical nickname. The seventh earl of Barrymore was known as 'Hellgate', a brother who was a compulsive gambler and threatened with imprisonment was called 'Newgate', the youngest brother who had a club foot was dubbed 'Cripplegate', and there was a sister 'whose savage temper and foul language combined to render "Billingsgate" an entirely appropriate soubriquet . . .'. (Quoted from Christopher Hibbert, *George IV: Prince of Wales*, London, Longman, 1972).

7

The Services have their own library of nicknames for commanders—a few of the more interesting are included in the dictionary—and for regiments, which are excluded because they have been well covered in the centenary edition of *Brewer's Dictionary of Phrase and Fable*, London, Cassell, 1970. Some personal nicknames have been public property: during the Boer War and after, everyone knew field marshal Lord Roberts, a great hero, as 'Bobs'. Not so well-known, except to his colleagues, was 'Pug' for general Lord Ismay who was chief of staff to the minister of defence in the Second World War and held high offices since. Even less well-known, and restricted to his staff, was 'Mary' for air marshal Sir Arthur Coningham under whom I served when he commanded a night bomber group and then when he was commander of second tactical air force during the invasion of occupied Europe, 1944–5. His was an example of how a nickname can be devised in a roundabout way. Sir Arthur was educated in New Zealand and served with the N.Z. forces in the First World War, and 'Mary' was a joking corruption of Maori.

Regimental nicknames often commemorate incidents in battle. The 'Cherry-pickers' were the 11th Hussars because they were taken unaware by French cavalry while gathering cherries in a Spanish orchard in 1811, but they fought back. When wounded at the battle of Albuera, the colonel of the 57th Foot urged his men to fight on and 'die hard', and so they did, and proudly adopted 'Die hards' as the nickname of the regiment. And the 15th Foot, fighting the Americans in the War of Independence, found their ammunition was running out so they clicked their muskets to make them sound as if they were firing, thus getting the nickname of 'the Snappers'. (This was at the battle of Brandywine in 1777 and their ruse was effective enough to contribute to the retreat of Washington's troops.) The 1st Dragoons, the 87th Foot and the Royal Scots Greys earned the nickname 'Birdcatchers' because they captured French eagle standards. These are just a few of many examples.

Another class of nickname which I have omitted—partly because most of the names are so familiar and obvious, partly because they have been exhaustively covered elsewhere—is the adjective-surname, the description with which the inventive mind has had great fun. Eric Partridge calls them 'inseperable nicknames'. These include 'dusty' Miller (because of the original miller's corn dust), 'spud' Murphy (the Irish being identified with potatoes), 'chalky' White, 'nobby' Clark (because clerks were at one time the 'nobs'—the nobility—to the labouring fraternity), 'dusty' Rhodes, and so on, and so on. Advertising has had its influence—Johnny goes with Walker of whisky fame, and Bob with Martin for a canine remedy. Children are adept at 'inseperables' and are continually adding to the collection. Two neat ones I have heard are 'turn-over' for a boy called Page, and 'spider' for a teacher called Webb.

For the record, as it were, let us also remember the nick-names for 'nationals', not included in the lists: Jock, Mack and Sandy for Scotsmen; Taffy the Welshman (from *Dafydd*, David); Mick the Irishman, Michael being so common a name there, as is Patrick (Paddy); Fritz the German; Frog or Froggy, because the English liked to believe that it was the Frenchman's favourite food, although they also gave him the nickname of Johnny (from *Jean*); Yank or Yankee q.v. for an American; and Ikey (Isaac) or Moses for a Jew.

Some cities have achieved nickname status: a few are noted here. But places and buildings have been left out because of their 'local' usage, such as Ally-pally for Alexandra Palace and Buck House for Buckingham Palace. Mention of these London landmarks reminds me of how nicknames crop up in the most unlikely places and how in research one thing leads to another. Searching for the origins of 'chitterlings', which began as a fashion nickname, I came across 'piccadils', a word I had forgotten, and from thence to Piccadilly Circus. This London location probably owes its identity to a nickname given to a mansion built by a certain Robert Baker in the early seven-teenth century. He amassed a little fortune out of tailoring, making and selling—among other things—the piccadil, or piccadilly, the high collar or ruff, often with perforated edging. The word comes from the French *picadille* (or *picoté*), meaning pricked. Mr Baker's neighbours may have thought him pre-tentious for a tradesman and invented the name Piccadilla Hall; or he may have thought of it himself. Then I found that Ivor Brown in *Chosen Words*, London, Penguin Books, 1961, acknowledged the nickname, and said that it applied to the whole estate. With his usual thoroughness, Mr Brown men-tioned another derivation—that, like the Tudor ruff, 'the area was then the fringe or necklet of the town, which still hugged the river between Westminster and the City'.

Trades and professions have their store of nicknames, for the implements they use and for the personalities within the confines of their craft. The staffs of the *Daily* and *Sunday Express* knew their chief as 'the Beaver', merited as much for Lord Beaverbrook's busy attention to his papers as for his name. And that great journalist Hannen Swaffer was known as 'the pope' or 'the bishop of Fleet Street', as a journalist of many years previously, Edward Sterling, was nicknamed 'the thunderer' q.v. when he wrote for *The Times*.

Tools of trade cannot be included: they are too esoteric. So are the nicknames for military weapons which have proliferated in two world wars and since—honest John, the US surface-to-surface rocket; bloodhound, the British anti-aircraft missile; Davy Crockett, the US short-range nuclear weapon; Tiny Tim, the American air-to-surface rocket; ferrets, the British armoured cars; kipper, a Russian weapon launched from the air against shipping; hound-dog, a US anti-submarine missile; and scores more. In the Second World War we called the Wellington bomber a 'wimpy', and the Halifax four-engine bomber the 'halibag'.

And what about gangsters and racketeers such as Al ('Scarface') Capone, notorious in the Chicago bootlegging days; 'Dutch' Schultz and 'Lucky' Luciano ('Public enemy number one')? As these are an American prerogative they are omitted. Britain has had no comparative gentry since the days of the highwaymen (some of whom are commemorated here), and it is the gang itself which has been given a nickname—a colourful outburst of them in the eighteenth century, subsiding in the latter part of the nineteenth (except for Ireland), and reviving in post-Second World War years.

In great contrast, what a delightful collection of botanical nicknames there are, inventions of folk-speech when most of us lived close to the countryside, unaware of the ponderous Latin classifications. How much prettier is forget-me-not than *myosotis arvensis*, and lady's slipper than *cyprepedium calceolus*, and the humble dandelion (*dent de lion*, because of the tooth-like edging to its leaves) than *taraxacum officinale*. What pleasanter nicknames could there be than lady's smock (or cuckoo flower), love in idleness, milkmaids, lords and ladies, touch-me-not, and London pride! And the names for butterflies that float around them—red admiral, Camberwell beauty, and the rest of the lovely lepidoptera.

The animal kingdom has its nicknames, also omitted here but familiar enough in junior schoolbooks—words like 'ship of the desert' for camel, 'king of the beasts' for lion, 'laughing jackass' for Australia's kingfisher. English, so far as I can find, has fewer nicknames for fish than has the French, which boasts such delightful ones as *ange de mere* for a kind of shark, and *loup de mere* for the sea bass.

Sport and entertainment

Sport has its nicknames, abounding in honorifics, and thereby precluding most—but not all—from this dictionary. They came into fruitfulness with the bare-knuckle fighters of the late eighteenth and early nineteenth centuries (and how gloriously evocative they were!) and have embellished the various branches of competitive contests ever since, especially cricket and tennis. But is it not strange that the two codes of rugby football, union and league, and association football which attract the greatest crowds (with hooliganism as well as fanaticism in the case of soccer) have so few memorable nicknames?

There are nicknames aplenty for teams, because of their grounds or the colour of their clothes—their 'strip'—but a scarcity for individual players. There are 'the Trotters' (Bolton Wanderers), 'the Avenue' (Bradford), 'the Mariners' (Grimsby Town), 'the Toffees' (Everton), 'the Shrimps' (Brighton), 'the Swans' (Swansea Town), 'the Spurs' (Tottenham Hotspur), 'the Wolves' (Wolverhampton), 'the Canaries' (Norwich City), 'the Blues' (Birmingham City), 'the Bees' (Brentford), to mention just a few; but where are the playing personalities? Their names are enshrined, but not nicknames, and the few there are have little distinction. The best that could be done for Sir Stanley Matthews, who played for England fifty-six times, was to call him 'the wizard dribbler'? Is it because of the nature of the game, and its following, or is it that football reporting lacks imagination and colour, and that writers of the quality of Neville Cardus, John Arlott and Hugh de Sélincourt and others skilled in the use of words have devoted their talents to cricket? Soccer has no literature comparable with that for cricket—or with boxing, for that matter.

Pugilistic nicknames were invented by 'the fancy' q.v., the coterie of promoters and backers of 'the noble art' q.v. who brought their champions 'up to scratch', that is, to the square or circle scratched on the ground to mark the arena, or the line in the middle of it. They go back to 'gentleman Jackson' and beyond: John Jackson was English champion for eight years from 1795. And there was 'west country Dick' who was beaten by Jack Randall, 'the prime Irish lad', the best light-weight of his time, also known as 'the nonpareil', over twenty-nine rounds in 1817. There was Jack Martin, called 'the baker' and 'master of the rolls' because of his trade, as was 'the gas-man' (Tom Hickman); 'the game chicken', 'black George' and a host of others, revered and feared, heroes of their age, the toast of the clubs, the friends of the sporting fraternity— the nobility among them—who not only wagered on their fights but sang their praises and wrote verses about them.

Pierce Egan, whose *Boxiana* was issued monthly between 1818–24, wrote lyrically of their fights and paid tribute to their characters, as did George Borrow to the 'bruisers of England' in *Lavengro*, and William Hazlitt in his essay 'The Fight', describing the eighteen-round contest between 'the gas-man' q.v. and Bill Neate in 1821. Was there ever, incidentally, a more bloodthirsty report of a boxing bout than Hazlitt's, or a more gory ending! Hickman's face 'was like a human skull, a death's head, spouting blood', yet he fought on until Neate knocked him senseless. Hazlitt must have had his tongue in his cheek when he introduced his essay: 'Ladies! it is to you I dedicate this description; nor let it seem out of character for the fair to notice the exploits of the brave!' Of such are heroes made— and nicknames, some of which will be found in the dictionary.

From 'gentleman Jackson' and 'Jem' (James) Belcher, whose last fight was with Tom Cribb in 1809, to 'gentleman Jim' (Corbett) who knocked out John L. Sullivan, 'the Boston strong boy', in 1892; from 'the brown bomber' (Joe Louis) to 'the Manassa mauler' (Jack Dempsey) and 'the magic man' (Lonnie Bennett); from 'Plum' (Sir Pelham) Warner, the cricketer, to 'Dolly' (Basil d'Oliveira) and the football knight, Sir Stanley Matthews—'the wizard dribbler'—who was presented with the freedom of his native Stoke-on-Trent, sporting nicknames have proliferated.

Cricket has had its generous share. There was that stalwart

of Broadhalfpenny Down in Hampshire ('the cradle of cricket') with the melifluous name of 'silver Billy Beldham' who lived to be ninety-eight, and his great all-round successor nearly a century later, the inimitable 'W.G.' (Dr William Gilbert Grace); those Australian fellers of English Test wickets, C. T. B. Turner ('the terror'), J. J. Ferris ('the fiend'), Frederick R. Spofforth ('the demon bowler'), and our own 'Ranji' (Kumar Shri Ranjitsinhji, who became the Maharajah of Nawanagar in 1906); and many a Yorkshire 'tyke' whose prowess has earned him a nickname on county grounds where cricket is almost a religion—'fiery Fred' Trueman among them. And, of course, one of the greatest of the batsmen, Australian Sir Donald George Bradman whom C. B. Fry dubbed 'the don'.

In tennis, 'gorgeous Gussie' Moran introduced frilly panties to Wimbledon, 'little Mo' Connolly thrilled the crowds, and Wimbledon itself was nicknamed 'Kingledon' q.v. because of Billie Jean King's domination of the ladies' singles for so long.

In the theatre, and especially the music-halls, honorifics have echoed the audiences' appreciation. What warmer expression of affection could have been given to Marie Lloyd than 'our Marie'? The only other performer to have received such an accolade is the inimitable Gracie Fields, 'our Gracie'. Few people in Edwardian England and for years afterwards were unaware that 'G.G.' could be no other than George Grossmith (Jnr.). Nicknames sometimes became professional names, like 'little Titch' q.v. who gave a word to the language. Often a nickname-stage name became inseperable from a performer, clearly identifying him—'the white-eyed kaffir' (G. H. Chirgwin), 'prime minister of mirth' (George Robey), among scores of examples on theatre billings.

Slang
There may be justifiable criticism that some words I have classed as nicknames are slang terms. The line of demarcation is often a thin one. I have had to make my own decision, working on the rough rule that if a questionable word has been accepted into what in Jane Austen's day and in Victorian parlance would have been described as 'polite society or conversation' then it has progressed into a nickname. In cases of doubt I have given the word the benefit of it, just as James

Barrie said he could not see a book lying lonely on a shelf without wanting to pat its back and give it sixpence.

Words have a habit over the centuries of slipping over the line to one side or the other. Take 'gob' as just one example. It was at one time a perfectly proper word for mouth, or mouthful, and it is still a respectable word in many dictionaries. Yet no one would maintain that the schoolboy's 'Shut your gob' is anything but slang. The first English 'gobet' for a morsel, or portion, was used by Chaucer in *The Canterbury Tales*, writing of the Pardoner:

> He seide he hadde a gobet of the seyl
> That saynt Peter hadde, when that he went upon the see.

Then there is 'cop' or 'copper' for a policeman, not included here because it is definitely slang, whereas 'bobby' and 'peeler' are nicknames for the same guardian of the law. And yet 'cop' in this sense, meaning to get or seize, probably comes from the very proper word 'copen', to buy or acquire, as used by John Lydgate (c1370–1451) when in *London Lickpenny* he writes:

> Where Flemings began on me for to cry,
> 'Master, what will you coppen or buy?'

And is it not strange that the slang expression 'He's copt it' (he has caught it, with the inference of punishment) is also used in the sense of 'He's bought it', the euphemism for death so familiar in the Second World War?

In the other direction there are many words once the slang of their day that have become respectable, and many former nicknames that have come to be accepted as honourable definitions in their own right: Methodists and Quakers (both q.v.) are two among scores, some of which are in these lists.

Slang has its own fascination and complicated ancestry, as Eric Partridge has demonstrated so brilliantly. It has its uses for emphasis in even the most serious discussions, as when Mr Enoch Powell, distinguished classical scholar as well as a member of parliament, and usually so correct in speech, said in a castigation of those who wished to remain in the 'common market' q.v. (17 May, 1975): 'Don't be silly, rub your eyes and use your loaf!' He was using rhyming slang—loaf of bread, head. He could just as easily have said 'nut', which is also slang for 'head', but which has an honourable antecedent, going back to Chaucer. Among the pilgrims to Canterbury was the yeoman—

A not-head hadde he with a broun visage.

Which means he was a nut-head, indicating respectfully enough that the yeoman's head and face were dark-coloured, probably with hair of a lighter hue on top, rather like an acorn or chestnut. Only later schoolboys transformed it into slang—'Hit him on the nut', 'crack his nut'. (Not to be confused with the other slang meaning for 'nut'—a dude, an elegant fellow: and also a crazy chap.)

These random examples show how living a thing language is, constantly renewing itself, as flexible a tool for thoughts as is the hand for the body. Not one aspect of it should be deplored; each contributes to the whole, whether it be the 'standard' English of Sir John Reith's BBC and professor Lloyd James, slang, jargon, cant, colloquialism and dialect.

Sometimes a distinction between a nickname and slang is a matter of personal feeling. Why do I think 'the box' is a legitimate nickname for a television receiver and 'goggle box' is slang; or why 'cissy' (like a sister) for an effeminate man should be avoided while 'cotquean' should not? And is 'gay' as a description of a homosexual a legitimate successor to 'ganymedes'?

I would like to have included all the many names for prostitutes, but most of these—like the Tudor 'hobby-horse' and 'abbess' for a brothel keeper—are too near to slang to qualify. A few of the more respectable have found a place.

In other words
Nicknames have a long and honourable history. They came before surnames, which were not common until the thirteenth century. And they provided many of those surnames as growing communities needed words of identification for their members. Kings could cling to their baptismal first names, and they could earn nicknames according to their abilities—or lack of them—or through physical features, during their reigns or posthumously; but commoners had to wrack their brains to extend the nomenclature from the obvious John the smith, Robin the miller, Peter the baker and so on, because a serf without a trade had no such claim on a designation. There might be

several Matthews and Marks, Toms and Timothys. It was easy enough to call Luke who made bows and arrows Luke the fletcher, so that he became Luke Fletcher and his descendants carried on the surname; similarly with Robin Miller, John Smith and the rest. Matthew might be dubbed 'bowman' because of his skill with the weapon, but the increasing numbers of Marks, Toms and Timothys had to be sorted out—one nick-named 'red-head', perhaps, another 'reed' because he was slim as such, and another 'brown' because of his dark skin, another 'broad-head'.

Smith and Smith's son (Smithson) were fine as far as they went and could establish their dynasty, but what of the black-smith's other sons? They had to devise, or be given, an identifi-cation: it could be another trade they followed, a position they held in the community, or they could take on the name of their village, especially if they moved away. (John Lydgate, for example, mentioned above, was born in the Suffolk village of Lydgate.) Or they could adopt a nickname, an extension of the first name to become a surname for posterity. My own name of Noble could either originate with an ancestor who was one— perhaps a Norman invader—or from a nickname designating the quality that the word implies, or because a forebear excelled in playing such a part in a pageant. (There was a Templar of that name as far back as the twelfth century, and vanity urges identification with an illustrious character rather than with a nickname based on the obsolete gold coin, the noble, worth 6s. 8d.!)

Having proved its value for personal identification, the nick-name was extended to groups of people (see 'lollards' and 'Wycliffites' as examples) and to places, seriously or amusingly, jostling with epithets to make a meaning clear or emphasise a characteristic, quality or particular type of allegiance. The weavers from Flanders who came over in groups to settle here in the middle ages needed no ingenious tag: they could all be classed as Flemings, contributing what became a common English surname. The later 'huguenots' q.v. were a different kettle of fish, because theirs was already a nickname and not from a country of origin, so they had to anglicize their names (see 'bowler'). Nicknames merge into words of convenience when it comes to identifying groups and sects and movements, a case of *multum in parvo*.

One wonders how many nicknames have been lost, how many convenient words used before the days of printing. Those of monarchs and monks, princes and prelates have survived from distant times; but what of those used in common speech by the farmer and corn-miller, the ale-wife and blacksmith, and an archer home from the wars? These must have enlivened conversation. Chaucer's pilgrims remind us of the home-spun wit that abounded. The 'ale-wife' herself, like 'ale-knight' and 'ale-stake', began as nicknames and are among the oldest we know; now they have been discarded. I have included many such half-forgotten words because of their place in linguistic history. If a saying such as 'take him down a peg' (see 'mug house') can survive for more than a thousand years, why should not an ancient nickname be recalled? Folk-speech retained many of these words until they could be written down, but probably only a small percentage.

The first journals and newspapers disseminated these jokers in the pack of words, so that they spread far afield from sophisticated London and the universities. From such publications came the recording—often the invention—of convenient terms to describe cumbersome titles, epochs, coteries and events. From the latter part of the seventeenth century inventiveness quickened so that new words were continually being added to the vocabulary, if not to the dictionary. The eighteenth century and the beginning of the nineteenth were productive periods, and there have been succeeding peaks and troughs. Two world wars stimulated invention, as did the rise of the 'popular' newspaper. Since 1950 the rate has quickened, even some acronyms being turned into words of convenience, which is something fairly new in language. Such combinations of letters as NATO, UFO, UNESCO, OPEC—lending themselves to easy pronunciation—have become words used in public speeches and in parliament, a feature of our restless language. Yet we have still to produce as ingenious a word as CABAL q.v., the initials of a five-man clique in the seventeenth century, or as POSH q.v.

So far as I can discover the two monarchs amassing most nicknames are Elizabeth I and George IV as prince, regent and king, rivalling Shakespeare; and the predominant groups to have been nicknamed or had convenient titles bestowed on them are religious sects, young reprobates and Irish gangs (the last named having such misleadingly attractive descriptions as 'peep o' day boys' and 'babes of the wood', both q.v.).

I am aware that nicknaming and antonomasia are closely linked and that much more attention could have been paid to the transference to somebody of the characteristics of a famous personage or figure from fiction—a Cicero for an orator, Bill Sykes for a thief. Shakespeare and Dickens have contributed most words of this kind—Shakespeare with his Dogberry q.v., among others; Dickens with his Pickwickian and Micawberish. I have made a selection from those in most general use— Adonis, Don Juan, for example—and from those that have lapsed in the passage of time but have an interesting background, like Bobadil.

The art of nicknaming—for that is what it seems to be— flourishes and expands with each day's newspaper when sub-editors searching for apt and attractive headlines invent concise descriptions for people and events. It is difficult to keep up with them and to decide which of the words is going to linger for more than a day and become established. One comes across few with the ingenious perfection of 'orange Peel' and 'Sinbad the tailor'; and I wish I knew who coined 'the perHapsburgs' for the later members of the Austro-Hungarian family in search of a throne.

In many a pub and club a new nickname has a closed-circuit vogue, is bandied about for a time, then forgotten. A few deserve a circulation. Among those I heard in 1975 were 'dismal Denis' (Denis Healey, chancellor of the exchequer), 'shiver-me-timbers Ted' (Edward Heath—an enthusiastic yachtsman in his spare time—when he lost the leadership of the Conservative party), the 'seventy-five dive' (for the drastic fall in the value of the pound), and 'Mr escort-me-out' (president Ford at the time of the controversy over withdrawal of US troops from Vietnam: only later generations may need to be reminded of the popular Ford car, the Escort). In the school playground the familiar nicknames persist—'lofty', 'shorty', 'sparrowlegs', 'ginger', 'bus' for a boy called Driver—but many have been updated: 'jet' for a fast runner, 'count-down(s)' for anyone whose surname is Down or Downes, 'lift-off' for a high jumper, and 'space-age' for a boy surnamed Sage.

Much of the etymology is my own and where not appropriately credited the excellent standard reference books must not be held responsible. The tracking of word origins is not the exact science that one might suppose, and there is often scope for speculation as to which language a word came from and how it was originally used, our own English being such an amalgam. It is a fascinating exercise to skip from one English dictionary to another—comparing the theories on sources—and then to German and French. Similarly one browses among encyclopaedias to determine how some nicknames arose, as well as keeping abreast of current newspapers and periodicals—and conversation. I hope this dictionary will stimulate further inquiry.

Note: the problem of keeping abreast of nicknames was emphasized by the popularity of 'the cod war'—denoting the fishing dispute between Britain and Iceland—after the list had been completed, and by Mr Denis Healey's gibe against some Conservatives in May 1976, calling them 'Tory Trots', likening them to Trotsky, the Russian revolutionary who supported Lenin but became critical of the regime. Sir Geoffrey Howe, Conservative 'shadow chancellor', referred to this latter as one of Mr Healey's 'curious little phrases', and commented: 'People who live in Marxist glass houses had better be pretty careful before they throw phrases like that around.'

A

abigail: a lady's maid, formerly a waiting gentlewoman, inspired by the story of Abigail, wife of Nabal whom David later married and to whom she said, 'Pray let your handmaid speak in your ears, and hear the words of your handmaid.' (I Samuel, xxv). Beaumont and Fletcher named a character after her in *The Scornful Lady*, 1610.

abolitionists: used for several reforming organisations, but generally applied to the late eighteenth-century movement led by William Wilberforce and others for abolishing the slave trade, culminating in an act of 1807. Later the term became familiar in English newspapers reporting the efforts in Australia to abolish the system of transporting convicts to New South Wales and Tasmania. Public pressure in Australia and Britain led to an end of transportation in 1853, after it had been in operation for sixty-five years.

abominable snowman, the: the yeti, unidentified creature of the Himalayas about which there are many legends, especially among the tribesmen of Nepal. It is said to have raided mountain villages and to be bearlike, with a near-human face, seven feet tall and powerful. Expeditions in the nineteen-fifties searched unsuccessfully, and in 1960 Sir Edmund Hillary ('Conqueror of Everest' with sherpa Tensing, 1953) found footprints which seemed to be those of an animal such as a bear. Windblown holes caused by rockfalls in the snow have been suggested as the origins of the tracks, but the legends of mysterious, isolated creatures high in the mountains persist.

Abraham men: demented beggars, later imposters; sometimes called 'Bedlam beggars'. Bethlehem Hospital (Bedlam), London, the first lunatic asylum in England, used as such from 1403, had wards named after saints and patriarchs, and inmates in Abraham ward being less violent than the others were allowed to go about the streets begging in the sixteenth and seventeenth centuries. They wore a badge of identification. Others unassociated with the hospital feigned lunacy and copied badges to attract public sympathy—and money. Shakespeare describes the beggars' behaviour in *King Lear* (II, iii) when Edgar says:

> Of Bedlam beggars who, with roaring voices,
> Strike in their numb'd and mortified bare arms
> Pins, wooden pricks, nails, sprigs of rosemary . . .

adamites: members of several sects from the second and third centuries on, originating in north Africa and spreading to Europe, aspiring to the innocence of Adam and therefore not subject to man-made laws. They defied conventions, including marriage, and discarded their clothes at religious meetings. They dwindled in numbers, occasionally revived, but in the fifteenth century public antipathy because of alleged crimes and immorality brought about their suppression. In England they called themselves 'brothers and sisters of the Free Spirit'.

Adam, the old: the wickedness within all of us; theologically, original sin.

Adam's ale, or **wine:** water.

Adam's apple: front-of-neck protruberance of the larynx, prominent in men; Latin, *pomum adami*. Also the lime and the orange because it was at one time suggested that these were more likely to have been the forbidden fruit in the garden of Eden.

Adam's profession: gardening, popularised by Shakespeare in *Hamlet* (V, i) when the First Clown says, 'There is no ancient gentlemen but gardeners, ditchers and grave-makers; they hold up Adam's profession'; and in 2 *King Henry VI* (IV, ii) when Jack Cade, in answer to a taunt about his lowly status, says, 'And Adam was a gardener.' Shakespeare took his cue from *Genesis*—'The Lord God took the man and put him in the garden of Eden to till it and keep it.'

admass: the advertising profession and the mass audience to whom its skills are directed, coined by J. B. Priestley in 1955 and taken up by many writers and journalists since, including Mary McCarthy in America, 1962.

Adonis: a dandy, a sartorially-conscious man or one who is handsome; from the beautiful youth in Greek mythology, beloved of Aphrodite. One of the several sarcastic nicknames given to George IV, although for the brief period in which it lasted it was more usually 'the fat Adonis' in the gossip of the clubs. See *Beau Brummell*; also *First Gentleman of Europe, Florizel, Fum the Fourth, Prinny*.

adullamites: Liberals who voted with the Tories in 1866 on a bill for extending the franchise and parliamentary reform. John Bright castigated them as retiring into the 'political cave of Adullam'. Those were the days of family Bible reading, when Bright's remark about the dissidents and their leader—likening them to the people who escaped with David to the cave of Adullam—would be understood: 'and everyone who was discontented gathered to him' (I *Samuel* xxii). The rebellious group was also known for a time as 'the cave'.

agony column: originally advertisements for missing people, lost property and animals, extended to letters from troubled readers and the first 'sob-sister' q.v. columns of advice to the love-lorn, etc. in magazines and newspapers.

albert: a short watch-chain fastened to a waistcoat button, as worn by Victoria's prince consort; also a kind of frock coat.

ale-knight: a drunkard or one who drinks beer heartily; cf. 'trencher-knight', q.v. Partridge *DSUE* traces the term to 1575. See also *maltworm*.

ale-stake: probably beginning as a nickname for the long pole projecting from a building denoting that it was a tavern or ale-house. If the former it might have had a garland or evergreen bush at the end of it, indicating that wine was also sold, hence the saying, 'A good wine needs no bush.' Such a sign appears to be on a building depicted in the Bayeux tapestry, evidence of its antiquity. There has long been in England another saying, 'Hang out the broom', meaning that there is an open-house, a welcome to everybody. Chaucer, describing the sompnour (summoner) in *The Canterbury Tales*, says:

A garland had he set upon his heed,
As gret as it were for an alé-stake

C. L. Duddington *Plain Man's Guide to Beer*, London, Pelham Books, 1974, points out that there were three types of hostelry —the inn, where accommodation as well as refreshment was provided; the tavern, which sold drinks and food; and the ale-house (also known as a 'tippling house' q.v.) which concentrated on ale (later beer, with the introduction of hops), probably brewed on the premises.

ale-wife: landlady of a tavern or ale-house. The sisterhood produced memorable characters, including a certain Mother Bunce of Cornhill, London, in the late sixteenth century, about whom there were many legends, crediting her with down-to-earth common sense and humour, recorded in print. She was even said to have lived to be 175! (The fish called an 'alewife' no doubt commemorates a landlady because of its plumpness.)

almighty dollar, the: international aspect of USA currency whose value dominated markets. See *petro-dollars*.

amazons: nickname for strong, muscular women, in sport or other activities; sometimes lightly used for female supremacy or success in a job or profession once the prerogative of men. The Amazons in Greek legend were a race of female warriors from Scythia, led by ruthless queens, allowing no men in their ranks and finding fathers for their children from other tribes, rearing only girls. They were said to cut off their right breasts so as to use their bows more efficiently—hence the Greek word for these magnificent women, *amazonides*, breastless.

ambling alp, the: Primo Canera (1906–67), Italian boxer, nearly six feet-six inches tall and weighing almost nineteen stones, world heavyweight champion from June, 1933 when he knocked out Jack Sharkey after six rounds, until June, 1934 when he was defeated by Max Baer in eleven rounds, both fights in New York. He boxed in England in 1929.

anderson: air raid shelter in the Second World War, named after Sir John Anderson who was home secretary and minister of home security, 1939–40. See *morrison*.

angry young men: 'protest' writers of the nineteen-fifties, showing a social awareness in their work, prominent among them being John Osborn, dramatist and actor, whose play,

Look Back in Anger, produced in 1956 (published 1957) inspired the name.

annus mirabilis: 1666, year of the great fire q.v. of London and English successes over the Dutch at sea, which John Dryden commemorated in a poem of this title. There have been other years so-named.

anthony eden: a black felt hat as worn by Sir Anthony Eden (later Lord Avon) when foreign secretary and one of the best-dressed members of the House of Commons in the nineteenth-thirties. He made the style fashionable. Cf. *bowler, Dolly Varden, Kevanhuller.*

Antonine's wall: earth rampart about thirty-six miles long which the Romans constructed, 140–1, between the Forth and Clyde in the reign of emperor Antoninus Pius. It was the northernmost outpost of Roman Britain. See *Hadrian's wall.*

anzacs: members of the Australian and New Zealand Army Corps who fought in the First World War and especially at Gallipoli, the name formed from the initials. Anzac Day in both countries is 25 April, commemorating the landing on the beaches exposed to Turkish fire in 1915.

armada, the: Spanish word outstanding in English history for the fleet of about 130 ships (many of them transport and not fighting vessels, galleys or small boats) sent by Philip II to conquer England in 1588. The expedition was commanded by the inexperienced duke of Medina Sidonia who hoped to be joined by the ships of the duke of Parma whose troops were waiting in Netherlands ports. The Spaniards had more armament than the English, but their gunnery was inferior, and the skill of the English commanders and sailors—under the general direction of lord high admiral Howard of Effingham—and help from the changing winds demolished the invaders. Gales finally wrecked many of the Spanish ships retreating by a northerly route. See *mosquito armada.*

ASH: appropriate acronym for the movement against cigarette smoking, Action on Smoking and Health, active in the nineteen-seventies because of the alarming increase in lung cancer.

ashes, the: since 1882 the symbol of Test match victory between English and Australian cricket teams. In that year the Australian team won for the first time in England by seven runs in an exciting game. The *Sporting Times* published a mock obituary notice with the words, 'In affectionate remembrance of English cricket . . . The body will be cremated and the ashes taken to Australia.' In the following winter England defeated Australia and retrieved its honour, whereupon some ladies in Melbourne burned straw and placed the ashes in a small urn and then presented it to the English captain, Ivor Bligh (later Lord Darnley) who took it back to Lord's cricket ground where it was given an honoured place in the pavilion. For more details see *M.C.C. 1787–1937*, London, The Times Publishing Company, 1937, and *Wisden*, 110th edn., London, Sporting Handbooks, 1973.

Athens of the north: nickname earned by Edinburgh as a seat of learning, with many long-established educational institutions and a university founded in 1583. Several European cities have from time to time been likened to the Greek capital with its ancient reputation for scholastic and artistic achievement, the most famous being Aachen in the days of Charlemagne who encouraged learning at his court and the revival of classical literature under Alcuin and others, 782 on. See *auld reekie*.

Augustan age: the golden age of Latin literature under Augustus Caesar when Horace, Ovid, Virgil, Livy and other writers flourished. Other countries have had their so-called Augustan age of literature, such as the period of Dryden to Dr Johnson in England, and that of Corneille, Molière and Racine in France.

auld reekie: descriptively affectionate name for Edinburgh from the eighteenth century because of its many smoking chimneys. Cf. *smoke, the* q.v.

auntie: the British Broadcasting Corporation, so dubbed mockingly by newspaper columnists and television critics, becoming familiar from 1954 at the start of commercial television, the BBC supposedly staid and unambitious by comparison. A BBC spokesman countered with, 'An auntie is often a much-loved member of the family.' The BBC assim-

ilated the nickname to such effect that when arrangements were made to supply wine to BBC clubs in London direct from vineyards in Burgundy it was bottled under the label *Tantine*. See *beeb*.

aussies: Australians.

authorised version, the: English translation of the Bible, authorised by James I, 1611, sometimes called 'the king's Bible'.

Ayrshire poet, the: Robert Burns (1759–96), born at Alloway, Ayrshire.

B

babes of the wood: Irish ruffians who ranged the Wicklow woods and mountains towards the end of the eighteenth century.

back bench: generic name for members of the House of Commons who sit on benches behind the government ministers and parliamentary secretaries, and those members on the opposition side whose seats are behind their leaders. See *front bench, left*, and *shadow cabinet*.

back o' beyond: any place remote from civilisation and inaccessible, probably originating from an Australian reference in the nineteenth century to the unexplored interior, 'the great outback'.

backroom boys, the: familiar in the services in the Second World War for scientists producing new gadgets or for planners of operations. Cf. *boffins* q.v. Lord Beaverbrook, when minister of supply, 1941, referred to 'boys in the back room'.

backstairs: indicating gossip or secretive influence, from the backstairs in royal apartments which gave private access to the monarch, used by courtiers and courtesans. On his coming

to the throne Charles I said that anyone who had business with him 'must never approach him by backstairs or private doors'. One of the many offices held by Pooh-Bah in *The Mikado* was groom of the backstairs.

bagman: commercial traveller, sales representative with samples in his bag. Partridge also defines it as an Australian colloquialism for a tramp. Cf. swagman.

baker, the: Louis XVI, because of the bread that he and Marie Antoinette (called 'the baker's wife') doled out to the mob at Versailles, 1789, and translated thus in English newspapers. (See also this nickname for Jack Martin, early nineteenth-century middleweight pugilist, Introduction p. 12.)

balaclava: a woollen head and cheeks covering, knitted in one piece after the style of a chain-mail helmet, popular with British troops in the cold of the Crimean War and named after the village where the famous charge of the Light Brigade took place, led by Lord Cardigan. See *cardigan, raglan.*

balmoral: a name very popular from the mid-nineteenth century when the prince consort bought Balmoral castle as a royal residence and given to various items of clothing, including a woollen cap in the Scottish fashion, a petticoat, women's laced bootees and men's shoes. The castle was acquired in 1848 and re-built a few years later in the baronial style, becoming a favourite holiday home for queen Victoria.

bamboo curtain, the: expressing the division between post-Second World War communist China and the western countries, similar in intent to the 'iron curtain' q.v. but with less general acceptance. The term was occasionally revived, as in *The Daily Telegraph,* 25 August, 1975: 'The week-end expulsion of foreign journalists from Bangladesh puts yet another Asian nation behind a bamboo curtain of news censorship.'

Banbury-man: a zealous puritan, because so many of this Oxfordshire town's citizens preached and practised their religious ideas and were satirised by seventeenth-century dramatists; thus the nickname was extended to mean a sanctimonious rogue and a hypocrite.

banting: a course of diet for weight-watchers which had a passing vogue among the Victorian middle class, excluding fats, starch and sugar, propounded by William Banting in a pamphlet, *A Letter on Corpulence*, 1863. He was a pioneer amateur dietician, and there is perhaps significance in the fact that he was an undertaker.

bard of Avon, the: William Shakespeare (1564–1616), one of the several names of tribute alluding to the river running through his birthplace at Stratford, such as 'sweet swan of Avon' (Ben Jonson's invention) and even 'Avonian Willy', credited to David Garrick.

barker: a fairground showman's front-man, drawing the crowds, attracting attention, or an auction tout; presumably likening him to a noisy dog.

barnstormer: a flamboyant or 'ham' actor with 'provincial' experience, from the strolling players who toured the country, performing in barns or on village greens, necessarily exaggerating their acting and delivery to suit their audiences and location.

Baxterians: followers of Richard Baxter (1615–91), eminent and controversial clergyman who was a chaplain in the Cromwellian army and to Charles II, in and out of favour in the Church of England, a prolific writer on religious subjects; an enemy of dissenting sects, especially the Quakers q.v. whom he called 'ignorant, proud, giddy sort of professors.' He was fined and imprisoned on a charge of sedition and libelling the church in his *Paraphrase of the New Testament*.

beatniks: young people who opted-out from normal society in the nineteen-fifties, unable or unwilling to cope with the stress of ordinary life, not conforming with conventional standards of thought, behaviour and dress, often getting into trouble with the law. The name was of American origin, indicating the 'beat' generation, with a Yiddish or Russian suffix (cf. the Russian *sputnik*, satellite orbiting the earth in 1957). One of a group of words for rebellious youth, such as 'teddy boys' q.v. preceding them and 'hippies' q.v. who followed, each with a different connotation.

Beau Brummell: George Bryan Brummell (1778–1840), leader of fashion in London society. His taste in clothes was evidenced at Eton and Oxford, and when he inherited a fortune he set himself up as an arbiter of male fashion, encouraged by his friends who also valued his witty conversation, his aplomb and conceit. The prince of Wales was one of his friendly admirers —for a time. He is credited with the rude remark about the future George IV, 'Who is your fat friend?' He lost his money by gambling and extravagance, and both his health and appearance deteriorated sadly. His nickname has been applied to a dandy or fop, but Brummell had an excellent sartorial taste.

Beau Nash: Richard Nash (1674–1762), famed as master of ceremonies at Bath which, under his strict and imaginative jurisdiction, enhanced its reputation as a fashionable spa. He went there after a brief army career and a study of law, took to gambling and seized the opportunities for his administrative skill so that he became known as 'the king of Bath'. He introduced rules for balls and assemblies, forbade the wearing of swords and boots in public places, brought duelling into disrepute, cleaned-up the streets and introduced a tariff for lodgings. His dress and trappings suited his status, wearing a large white hat and richly embroidered coat, and driving about town in a carriage with six horses and uniformed grooms blowing French horns.

beaver: both a hat (of beaver fur, providing a great market in Britain for the trappers of the Hudson's Bay Company in north America from the seventeenth century on) and a beard because of its furry aspect.

bedchamber affair (or crisis), the: a political furore in 1839 when Sir Robert Peel succeeded Lord Melbourne as prime minister and demanded that some of the whig ladies of the bedchamber be replaced by those of tory inclinations. Queen Victoria refused and he resigned.

beeb, the: facetious nickname for the British Broadcasting Corporation (BBC) introduced by critics and columnists of the 'popular' papers, but also taken up by more sober journals. Typical is from the London Letter of *The Guardian*, 7 March, 1975: 'Several readers have drawn my attention to Clive Jenkins's outrageous remarks on the Beeb earlier this week...'

Two nicknames were used in *The Observer*, 11 May, 1975: 'Mr Tony Benn's blistering attack on the BBC . . . has opened up some sore old wounds in the fight between the Labour Party in the red corner and Auntie Beeb in the blue.' See *auntie*.

beefeaters: Yeomen of the Guard who have attended state occasions from the coronation of Henry VII in 1485. Their duties included being at royal banquets at which they probably tucked into the 'left-overs'. They would have had access to the kitchens and be given a generous food allowance, hence the nickname for well-fed state servants. Warders at the Tower of London have also been known as beefeaters since the seventeenth century. Cf. note to 'doughboy' on the coincidence of that name with soldiers' payment in food.

belcher: a blue scarf with white spots, current from the early nineteenth century because such neckwear was sported by James (Jem) Belcher (1781–1811), a pugilistic favourite during his short career. His last fight in 1809 was with Tom Cribb who defeated him. He had been a butcher, but he retired from the ring to become a publican.

Belisha beacon: a yellow glass globe atop a pole marked in black and white bands and situated on both sides of a pedestrian crossing as a warning to motorists; introduced when Leslie Hore-Belisha (created a baron, 1954) was minister of transport, 1934–7. See *zebra crossing*.

bellman: a night-watchman calling the hours (and often the state of the weather) and a town crier, summoning people with his bell to hear announcements and advertisements.

bell-the-cat: Archibald Douglas, fifth earl of Angus (c1450–1514) who earned the nickname by devising a scheme to get rid of Robert Cochrane, hated favourite of James III of Scotland. He is reputed to have said that he would 'bell the cat', and he began the attack by pulling Cochrane's gold chain from his neck. Cochrane and others were hanged. Douglas switched his allegiance, and was a leader in the rebellion against James.

below stairs: both the servants' quarters and the hierarchy of domestic service in large houses, usually excluding the butler, valet and 'nanny'; the stairs being those from the basement and (or) those to the reception rooms on the first floor.

benedick: a newly-married man—despite his protestations against women, as Benedick changed his tune in *Much Ado About Nothing:* 'I did never think to marry . . . I have railed so long against marriage . . . When I said I would die a bachelor I did not think I should live till I were married.' (II, iii.)

Benicia boy, the: John C. Heenan, American boxer from Benicia in California, who in 1860 fought for more than two hours with Tom Sayers, the English champion. The contest ended in a draw after thirty-seven rounds. Sayers, who had been beaten only once in his long career, retired after this fight.

Bennery: the socialist policies of Anthony Wedgwood Benn when minister of state for industry, including nationalisation, perhaps coined by Nicholas Ridley, conservative M.P. who, in a letter to *The Daily Telegraph,* 17 May, 1975, wrote, 'Indeed it is hard to see how people are going to be persuaded to leave the public sector . . . and return to the private sector where (Bennery aside) they have to earn their own livings by competitive endeavour.' See *Wedgie.*

Bevin boys: young men directed to work in the coal mines as a wartime measure when Ernest Bevin was minister of labour and national service, 1940–5. See *dockers' K.C.*

big Ben: the bell in the clock tower of the Houses of Parliament, London, weighing thirteen-and-a-half tons, named after Sir Benjamin Hall, commissioner of works when it was hung in 1856. Under the heading CLOCKING IN *The Northern Echo* 26 January, 1976, reported: 'Big Ben rang out again yesterday after a brief rest for decoration.'

big Bertha: soldiers' nickname for the German long-range gun in the First World War, used to shell Paris in 1918. Bertha, only child of Friedrich Alfred Krupp (1854–1902) who had inherited the great engineering and armaments undertaking, married in 1906 and her husband became head of the firm.

32

big brother: watchful officialdom, dictatorial in its powers, from the sinister omnipotent leader of a subservient country in George Orwell's *Nineteen-Eighty Four*, a novel which had a considerable impact when published in 1949.

big smoke, the: see *smoke*.

big three, the: Churchill, Roosevelt and Stalin, heads of the UK, USA and Russian governments in the Second World War, so called when they met in conference at Yalta, 1945.

big top, the: the large tent for performances in a touring circus, often transferred to the circus itself.

bigwig: a man of importance or holding a position of authority, from the seventeenth- and eighteenth-century fashion among the middle classes of wearing large wigs. The fashion declined in the latter half of the eighteenth century, as did the size of wigs, but persisted in the case of such high officials as judges, the speaker of the House of Commons and the lord chancellor who wore 'full-bottomed' wigs, while barristers sported the smaller or 'tie wig'.

billingsgate: coarse language, as used in London's famous fish market, the city's oldest market, becoming such in 1699. (The name comes from an ancient British king, Belin, who built a tower with a gate in it near the site.) Old Mr Osborne in Thackeray's *Vanity Fair* (ch. xiii), 'made a few curt remarks respecting the fish . . . and cursed Billingsgate with an emphasis quite worthy of the place'. See also Introduction, p. 7.

black country: an area in the English midlands, including south Staffordshire and parts of Warwickshire and Worcestershire where coal mines, iron works and factories besmirched the landscape and their smoke polluted the atmosphere, from the industrial revolution on.

black death, the: bubonic plague which ravaged Asia and then Europe in the fourteenth century, a symptom being the discoloration of the skin. Millions of people died, and in London alone it was estimated that 50,000 succumbed. The next great outbreak in Britain, 1665–6, was more precisely recorded. See *great plague*.

black diamonds: coal, because of its great value to industry and domestic heating, and both the fuel and the gem are of carbon.

black diamond, the: Tom Cribb (1781–1848), English pugilist who was a coal-porter. He defeated Jem Belcher twice and the American negro, Tom Molineaux. He was greatly admired for his skill, strength and sportsmanship, and was said to possess 'great forbearance of temper'.

black Douglas: James, lord of Douglas (1286–1330), so called by the English for his raids on the border, and perhaps because of the way he captured Roxburgh castle in 1314 by disguising his men as black oxen. Two years later he slew Sir Robert de Nevill, 'peacock of the north', in single combat. He fought on the side of Robert Bruce and is romanticised in Scottish history for his dash and daring. He died fighting the moors in Spain. There is an interesting 'black' connection with the noble family of Douglas, the name originating from the Gaelic *dubh glas*, dark water.

black Friday: Good Friday of the Easter festival, when congregations wore mourning for the crucifixion of Jesus and the altar was draped in black.

black gold: negro slaves, the slave trade bringing great riches to those who participated in it.

black hole: a region of space into which a star has collapsed, and from which nothing—not even light—can escape, the conclusive proof for which began to exercise the minds of astronomers in the nineteen-seventies. The theory was that the gravitational pull of the collapsed star was so great that although light could enter the 'forbidden zone' around it could not get away. Such a star is extremely massive, and when it began to collapse by gravitational forces, following the cessation of its nuclear reactions, there was nothing capable of halting the process. A star of lesser mass would explode as a supernova and end as a pulsar (neutron star), plus a cloud of expanding gas; one of still lower mass, such as the sun, would collapse into a 'white dwarf' star made up essentially of degenerate matter.

black hole (of Calcutta): a cell in the East India Company's fort at Calcutta into which 146 European prisoners were

34

crammed when captured by the nawab of Bengal's troops, 1756. The cell, or guardroom, measured about eighteen by fifteen feet and was perhaps eighteen feet high (various dimensions have been given), and the June heat was intense. There were only two small windows. Only twenty-three prisoners, including one woman, had survived by next morning.

black Jack: John Philip Kemble (1757–1823), handsome, dark-haired actor, brother of Mrs Siddons, noted for his tragic Shakespearean characters, including Hamlet. He became manager of Drury Lane and Covent Garden theatres.

black maria: police van, painted black. There has been much speculation about 'maria'. It may be connected with the notorious murder of a girl called Maria Marten, for which a man was hanged in 1828. Maria and the red barn in which her body was found became subjects of plays and stories, and the most notable melodrama, produced in London in 1840, is part of theatrical history. An American explanation for the name is that a brawny negress called Maria who kept a lodging house in Boston helped the police to bundle arrested people into the van.

Laurie Dickson, assistant to Thomas Edison, used the nickname in a very different way. 'It was not until 1893 that Dickson built what was probably the first movie studio ... called the "Black Maria", because it was a shed painted black inside and out; it rested on a revolving base which could turn to follow the sun and keep the actors brightly lighted against black backgrounds.' Frederic M. Thrasher, *Okay for Sound*, New York, Duel, Sloan and Pearce, 1946.

black market: the acquisition and sale of goods outside legal restrictions during periods of shortage, as in wartime, consequently at prices higher than those regulated by rationing; also the unofficial market for anything when demand exceeds supply, such as tickets for sporting events. See *spiv*.

blackout, the: familiar to civilians in wartime to describe the period of darkness when no lights were to be displayed for fear of attracting enemy bombers. It was particularly widespread and severe in the Second World War when blinds and curtains were drawn over windows, car and street lamps masked, and wardens made inspections to ensure that no glimmer of light could be seen from above. The term was taken into peacetime parlance, as the headline in *The Times*, 6 May, 1975: 'Blackout threat by power men to support wages claim.'

black prince, the: Edward, prince of Wales (1330–76), eldest son of Edward III. He fought with distinction at the battles of Crécy and Poitiers and gained his nickname because of his black armour.

blackshirts: uniformed fascist followers of Benito Mussolini in Italy and of Adolf Hitler in Germany, but usually applied to the former who became active in the nineteen-twenties: Hitler's blackshirts (the SS) came into prominence in the nineteen-thirties. The black shirt became a symbol of fascism, and in England it was worn by followers of Sir Oswald Mosley who re-formed his New Party into the British Union of Fascists. See *blueshirts, brownshirts, redshirts.*

blanketeers: Lancashire handloom weavers, spinners and other cotton and wool operatives, impoverished by changing industrial conditions, who assembled on St Peter's field, Manchester (later scene of the Peterloo massacre q.v.) in 1817 to march to London to petition the prince regent. Each carried a blanket for the planned several days' journey. They did not get far, however, before their ranks were broken up by the authorities, and they were eventually dispersed at Derby, their leaders later imprisoned.

blighty: British soldiers' reference to the home country when serving abroad, originating in India from a Hindustani word, used extensively in the First World War but not so much in the Second. A 'blighty wound' was one severe enough to take the soldier back to Britain for treatment or convalescence.

blimp: observation balloon or non-rigid airship in the First World War, and a balloon guarding specific targets from low-level air attack in the Second. The airship was classified as B-limp. Cartoonist David Low created colonel Blimp, an inflated gentleman with dogmatic old-fashioned views, representing a die-hard tory.

blitz: a sudden and concentrated attack by ground and/or air forces as practised by the Germans in the Second World War,

36

from *blitzkrieg*, 'lighting war'. It was most commonly used for Luftwaffe bombing attacks on London and other cities. In a profile on playwright Harold Pinter, who was evacuated from London to Cornwall in 1939, in *The Observer*, 27 April, 1975: 'A year or so later, during a lull in the Blitz, he was reclaimed by his mother.'

blockbusters: nickname given by RAF crews to the heavier bombs which could be carried when Halifax and Lancaster four-engine bombers came into service, especially the first four-thousand-pounders; followed by even more powerful and devastating 'cookies'.

bloody assizes, the: trials in the west of England of those concerned in the uprising led by the duke of Monmouth who claimed the throne after the death of Charles II in 1685. Judge Jeffreys presided and inflicted severe sentences. It has been estimated that more than three hundred people were condemned to death: Monmouth was beheaded.

bloody butcher, the (or butcher of Culloden): the duke of Cumberland because of his cruelty in dealing with the Jacobites q.v. at and after the battle of Culloden, 1746.

bloody Mary: Mary I (1516–58), daughter of Henry VIII and Catherine of Aragon, who re-established Roman Catholicism during her short reign and there was persecution of protestants: about 300 were executed.

bloomers: a female fashion of a skirt reaching to just below the knees and under which were wide trousers, gathered at the ankles. A close-fitting jacket usually completed the ensemble. The fashion was introduced in New York by Mrs Amelia Jenks Bloomer in 1851, and it was soon adopted in England where it had a sensational vogue for a time and delighted cartoonists. The trousers were especially appropriate for younger ladies taking up the recreation of bicycling, and the word became a nickname for these nether garments, then as they disappeared under longer skirts it was applied to the underwear which for long preceded knickers and panties.

Bloomsbury group (circle or set): a coterie of literary and artistic people who lived in and around that district of London before and after the First World War, meeting to discuss their own and others' work, including Leonard and Virginia Woolf, Maynard Keynes, Lytton Strachey, Roger Fry, Morgan Foster, Duncan Grant, Vanessa and Clive Bell. The original members were known to initiates as 'old Bloomsbury'. See Leonard Woolf, *Downhill All the Way*, London, The Hogarth Press, 1967.

bluchers: leather half-boots, either because field marshal Gerhard L. von Blücher, the dashing old commander of the Prussian army at Waterloo, wore them, or in association with 'wellingtons' q.v. In his *Name Into Word*, London, Secker and Warburg, 1949, Eric Partridge gives it as slang for cabs which picked-up passengers at London stations after all the privileged cabs (those allowed on the ranks) had been hired, in allusion to Blucher's late arrival for the decisive battle against Napoleon. Blucher's own nickname was 'marshal *vorwarts*' (forward!).

bluejackets: British sailors, from the nineteenth century. Colour of uniforms has produced many nicknames: cf. 'redcoats' q.v. and the various 'shirts'. Federal soldiers of the American civil war were called 'bluebellies' by the confederates because of their light blue overcoats and cloaks, and in return the latter were named 'greybacks', alluding to their grey uniforms. An RAF nickname for a khaki-clad soldier was 'brown job'.

blue pencil: censorship, restrictions, deletions; originating as a journalistic term for editors' or sub-editors' cancellation of copy, marked with such a pencil. The association of blue with censorship—and hence by inversion with obscenity and sex (such as 'blue jokes', 'blue films')—goes back a long way, perhaps to seventeenth-century New England when Puritan magistrates promulgated what were known as 'blue laws' (was it because they were printed in blue?) to enforce church attendance and moral standards, especially in New Haven, Connecticut. Public and private behaviour, even dress, were regulated: adultery was punishable by death. In England, the first Monday before Lent used to be called 'blue Monday' because workmen spent it in dissipation.

blue-ribbonites: nineteenth-century crusaders against intoxicating liquor, identified by a piece of blue ribbon on their coat lapels, blouses or arms—as well as by their preaching fervour. They were known as the blue ribbon army, founded in America and spreading to Britain where in 1883 it took the name of the Gospel Temperance Union.

blueshirts: Irishmen who volunteered to fight for general Franco in the Spanish Civil War, 1936–9.

bluestockings: literary or studious women, from the gatherings of cultivated females and a few eminent men who met in various places but especially at the home of Elizabeth Montagu in Mayfair, London, a leader of society who encouraged discussion of the latest books and poems instead of banter and gossip over games of cards. These intellectual conversaziones began around 1750 and the playful nicknames of 'bluestocking ladies' and 'bluestocking clubs' are explained by Boswell in his *Life of Johnson*. He says that a certain Benjamin Stillingfleet, expert on natural history, was a popular guest, soberly dressed but wearing blue stockings. 'Such was the excellence of his conversation, that his absence was felt as so great a loss, that it used to be said, "We can do nothing without the blue stockings", and thus by degrees the title was established.' Dr Johnson, who was very fond of the ladies, attended the sessions himself. It is also said that Mrs Montagu and her coterie took to wearing blue stockings.

The influences of female critics continued long after her death in 1800, because Byron mocked them in *Don Juan*, iv, 108–112:

> Oh! ye who make the fortunes of all books!
> Benign Ceruleans of the second sex!
> Who advertise new poems by your looks,
> Your 'imprimatur' will ye not annex?

and later:

> They say your stockings are so—(Heaven knows why.
> I have examined few pairs of that hue);
> Blue as the garters which serenely lie
> Round the patrician left-legs, which adorn
> The festal midnight, and the levée morn.

boar, the: Richard III (1452–85), because of the boar on his heraldic cognizance; also called 'crookback' q.v. See also *Lovell the dog*.

boater: a shallow-crowned straw hat with flat brim, as worn at Harrow school and adopted by fashionable late Victorian and Edwardian men in their punts and other river boats.

bobadil: a military boaster, now down-at-heel, bragging of his exploits, as captain Bobadil in Ben Jonson's *Every Man in his Humour* (a comedy in which Shakespeare acted), 1598. He was also referred to as a Paul's man q.v.

bobby: policeman, from Sir Robert Peel who as home secretary established the metropolitan police force in 1829. The nickname 'peeler' q.v. was introduced from Ireland. See also *charlies, redbreasts.*

bobby-soxers: American schoolgirls and older teenagers who adopted white short socks in the nineteen-forties. Such socks, short or long, were identified with exuberant youth for several years, and the British press used the name for noisy teenagers at dances and early post-war 'pop' concerts.

Bobs: Frederick Sleigh Roberts (1832–1914), created earl Roberts, one of the most popular of British soldiers with over forty years' service in India, including distinction in the Mutiny (for which he was awarded the VC) and his famous march from Kabul to Kandahar. In 1900 he took command of the British forces in South Africa and brought the Boer War to an end. (His only son was killed in this war.) He was received by queen Victoria at her last audience before her death.

boffins: scientists and experimenters, probably of RAF invention but adopted in other services; a word often used in briefing air crew on navigational aids, bomb-aiming, gunnery, etc. There was an eccentric gentleman called Mr Boffin in Dickens's *Our Mutual Friend.* Cf. *backroom boys* q.v.

bogeys: the 'blips' on a radar screen which denoted enemy aircraft (from 1939), marking them off from 'our own' bombers and fighters by iff (identification, friend or foe). See *radar.*

boneshaker: early bicycle before the days of pneumatic tyres and spring saddles; or any vehicle that rocks and rolls.

Boney: Napoleon Bonaparte (1769–1821), from 1798 when it seemed that he was threatening an invasion of Britain, used in derision or to keep our courage up. See *corporal violet* and *little corporal*.

boniface: an innkeeper, from the landlord in George Farquhar's comedy *The Beaux' Stratagem*, 1707.

bonnie prince Charlie: see *young pretender*.

Boston tea party, the: the incident in Boston harbour, USA, 16 December, 1773, when citizens dressed as Indians flung three cargoes of tea from British ships into the sea as a protest against the tea act of that year.

Boswell, a: a biographer, especially a rather slavish and adulatory one, as was James Boswell, adoring biographer of Dr Johnson. See *Bozzy*.

bottom drawer: the assembly of clothes and domestic linen made by a woman in preparation for her marriage. Such necessary garments and furnishings were usually stored in the bottom drawer, because in most chests of drawers this was the deepest one.

bowler: a low-crowned hard hat, introduced by William Coke of Norfolk in 1850 to replace his high riding hat as more suitable for hunting, a kind of neat crash helmet designed by a well-known hatter, Mr Beaulieu, one of a family of such craftsmen in Stockport and London who anglicised their Huguenot name to Bowler. The hat was sometimes called a 'coke', sometimes a 'billycock', both after the Norfolk gentleman. In America the hat got the name of 'Derby' when it was observed from pictures that Lord Derby invariably wore one at races and other public occasions.

A catch-phrase, 'Getting his bowler hat', developed in the armed services, indicating dismissal or retirement, because it became the customary civilian headgear of Guards officers on leave and of those retiring to 'civvy street'.

bowler-hatted bull: farmers' nickname for a ministry of agriculture representative or veterinary surgeon who artificially inseminates cows.

Bow street runners: see *redbreasts*.

box, the: a television receiver, nickname in general use from the nineteen-fifties, the slang version for which was 'goggle box'; frequently employed by newspaper television critics in the phrase 'on the box', referring to a programme.

Bozzy: Dr Johnson's playful nickname for James Boswell (1740–95), his friend and biographer. Bozzy's fame rested almost entirely on his *Life of Johnson*, first published in 1791, until the discovery of his diaries and journals and their publication from 1950 on.

bradburies: treasury notes, especially one-pound notes, signed by J. S. Bradbury, joint permanent secretary to the treasury, 1913–19. It is difficult to explain why no other signature on paper money achieved such nickname fame. His successor, Norman Fisher, provided 'fishers' but it was by no means so catching.

brandy Nan: queen Anne (1665–1714), presumably because she was fond of it; but she was also fond of tea, as in the couplet—

> Here thou, great Anna! whom three realms obey,
> Dost sometimes counsel take—and sometimes tea.

She liked to call herself Mrs Morley when she gossiped with Sarah Churchill, duchess of Marlborough, who took the pseudonym of Mrs Freeman and was nicknamed by courtiers, 'queen Sarah' q.v. because of her influence.

brass hat: high ranking military officer because of the gold-metal oak leaves on his cap, the nickname persisting from the Boer War through the two World Wars and after. The collective nickname is 'top brass'. In the RAF the gold insignia for group captains upwards was known as 'marmalade' and 'scrambled eggs'.

brewer, the: Oliver Cromwell (1599–1658), gibe by the royalists from the belief that when a youth he helped his widowed mother in a brewery business. See *nosey*.

bride of the sea: one of the many honorifics for Venice which became well-known in eighteenth-century England when the 'grand tour' q.v. had really got into its stride. It arose from the annual ceremony on ascension day when the doge, in his state barge, threw a ring into the water to symbolise the city's marriage with the sea, a custom initiated by pope Alexander

III in 1174. Venice was notorious among the gentry, as the many diaries show, and must have been a topic of conversation, not only because of its architecture and carnivals but because of its general reputation for high jinks, earning it another nickname, 'the brothel of Europe', so many prostitutes being available. The stench and the dirt of the place, recorded by tourists, and the sharp practices by tradesmen contrasted oddly with the honorifics, which included 'gem of the Adriatic'.

bright young things: young socialites of the nineteen-twenties and early 'thirties whose reaction to the rigours of recent war was to be gay and dance and give parties, copied in more modest style by their poorer compatriots. They lived in a short period of frivolity, disregarding the poverty and unemployment around them, flouting convention and dancing the charleston. 'One of the Bright Young Things in that brilliant and stimulating era between the wars', from the dust cover of Alec Waugh, *A Year to Remember*, London, W. H. Allen, 1975. See *roaring twenties*.

Bristol boy, the: Thomas Chatterton (1752–70), talented young poet who began writing verse at the age of ten and in his short life produced some remarkable work, including a so-called discovery of ancient poems and prose, later proved a fake, but attractive nevertheless. He committed suicide in a London garret.

British Solomon, the: James I (1566–1625), an honorific matched only by the sycophantic dedication to him of the 'authorised version' q.v. of the bible, a gem of flattery—'Your very name is precious ... the zeal of Your Majesty towards the house of God doth not slack ... manifesting itself abroad in the farthest parts of Christendom ...' The nickname referred to his writings, including his *Daemonologie*, a denunciation of witchcraft, and contrasted sharply with another one, 'the wisest fool in Christendom'.

brown bess: the old flintlock musket of the British army, because of its colour. It was introduced in the eighteenth century and was still in use at Waterloo, 1815.

brown bomber, the: American boxer Joe Louis who was world heavyweight champion, 1937–49.

brownshirts: civilian army formed by Adolf Hitler and which British visitors to Germany from the early nineteen-thirties found in town and city streets, and marching and drilling in the countryside, wearing a uniform of brown shirt with swastika armband, and breeches. See *blackshirts, blueshirts, redshirts.*

Bryanites: followers of William O'Bryan (1778–1868) who founded a group calling themselves Bible Christians. He had joined the Wesleyan church, but was expelled in 1810 after arguments about discipline.

Brylcreem boys, the: young officers in the RAF in the early part of the Second World War, especially those who had joined the RAFVR, facetiously given this nickname (mainly by soldiers) because one such was pictured in advertisements for a popular brand of hair cream (with this name and spelling.)

Buchmanites: followers of Frank N. D. Buchman (1878–1961), American who founded an ideological movement first known as the Oxford Group q.v., then from 1938 as Moral˙ Re-armament (MRA), based on Christian beliefs and with ethical aims non-sectarian in appeal; international and anti-communist, seeking to reconcile opposing factions in industry and politics, advocating that an individual must change himself in order to change nations and affairs.

Buffalo Bill: William Frederick Cody (1846–1917), American showman who took the name from his days as a buffalo hunter to provide meat for workers on the Kansas Pacific railway. His adventurous life began as a rider in the 'pony express' mail service. He became a scout and guide for the US army, then served with the Kansas cavalry in the Civil War, later taking part in the Indian wars and killing the Cheyenne chief Yellow Hand in single combat. He organised his first 'wild west' show in 1883, with cowboys and Indians, and brought it to England in 1887 with spectacular success.

bulldog breed, the: name accepted by the British people for their strength and tenacious characteristics, likened to one of the oldest of distinctive British dogs, bred for bull-baiting. (Now through interbreeding the bulldog has become good-natured and docile, and by no means as fearsome as it looks.)

bullfrog of the Pontine marshes: Benito Mussolini (1883–1945), so named derisively by Winston Churchill in the Second World War. Churchill despised the Italian dictator.

Burlington Harry: Henry Flitcroft (1697–1769), joiner-turned-architect who designed London churches (St Giles-in-the-Fields, St Olave's, Southwark) and worked on great houses such as Woburn Abbey. His patron was Lord Burlington for whom he designed Burlington House in London.

Busby's babes: younger members of Manchester United football team whose manager, Matt (later Sir Matthew) Busby coached and encouraged into a winning side after the tragic loss of experienced players in an air crash at Munich, 1958.

butcher of Culloden: see *bloody butcher*.

C

cabal: perhaps the first acronym to become a dictionary word, meaning a clique or secret body, derived from the five initials of Lords Clifford and Arlington, the duke of Buckingham, Lord Ashley and the duke of Lauderdale whom Charles II formed into a kind of cabinet in 1672.

canter: a word invented from the name of a town, approaching nickname status, indicating the easy jog-trot of a horse, the ambling pace at which pilgrims undertook the journey to the shrine of Thomas Becket at Canterbury, as Chaucer's company 'that toward Caunterbury wolden ryde'; sometimes called 'the Canterbury gallop'.

canucks: Canadians, especially those of French descent, probably from Chinook, an Indian tribe that traded with the Hudson's Bay company.

capability Brown: Lancelot Brown (1715–83), architect and landscape gardener who revived the naturalistic style of estate planning, with long vistas from the mansion windows,

45

tastefully arranging trees, lakes and flower beds. He was commissioned to plan gardens at Blenheim and Kew among other large estates. His nickname came from his comment after a survey, 'It's capable' or 'It has great capabilities.'

captain Swing: a name used by agricultural workers in the southern counties in their threats against farmers and landowners when there was great discontent about conditions and the introduction of machinery around 1830. For two or three years the instigators of violence hid their identity under this pseudonym. See also *luddites.*

cardigan: a woollen waistcoat, as worn by British soldiers in the Crimean war and named after the earl of Cardigan who commanded the Light Brigade at Balaclava. See also *balaclava.*

carpet-baggers: north American political and commercial adventurers who went south after the civil war, taking over many of the leading offices with the help of the negro vote and reaping riches for themselves. The term was adopted in Britain for an opportunist adventurer, but did not retain a firm hold.

carpet knight: a titled 'softie', having been awarded a knighthood without distinction in combat—dubbed at court instead of on the field of battle. The nickname originated in the sixteenth century, and was later extended to indicate a philanderer, braver in the boudoir than in battle.

Casanova: a merited or self-described flirt with remarkable sexual prowess, similar to Casanova de Seingalt (1725–98), Italian adventurer and philanderer, who boasted of his conquests. He was a skilful 'con man' of many talents among the courts and aristocracy of Europe (including England), apart from his amorous exploits which he recounted in an autobiography.

Cassandra: a foreteller of doom, hence a pessimist, after the legendary Greek prophetess of events (usually disastrous), although Apollo arranged that no one believed her.

cat's whisker: the spiral of fine wire directed to a sensitive spot on a crystal to receive radio signals, familiar to everyone who made his own 'crystal set' from the start of public broadcasting in 1922 before going on to valves.

cavaliers: royalists, supporters of Charles I in the struggle with the parliamentarians. The first parliament after Charles II's restoration was called 'the cavalier parliament'. It was the counter nickname of 'the roundheads' q.v. for the royalists, and according to Antonia Fraser, *Cromwell Our Chief of Men*, London, Weidenfeld and Nicolson, 1973, 'originally derived from the Spanish word *caballeros* and mocked the alleged allegiance of the English court to foreign Catholic ways.'

charlies: night watchmen, from the seventeenth century, probably because it was under Charles I that a system of policing the streets was regularised. See *bobby, peelers, redbreasts*.

chartists: members of a political movement of working class origin beginning in 1838, with a charter of desired reforms including the abolition of property qualifications for MPs and payment for their services, manhood suffrage and vote by ballot, and annual parliaments. A petition signed by more than a million people was submitted in 1839, but ignored; and another was prepared in 1848, the plan being to march to the House of Commons to present it, but troops made the procession impossible. See *year of revolutions*.

children of Mercury: scholars, travellers and tradesmen because the Mercury of Roman mythology was identified with the Greek Hermes who was the most versatile of gods, giving his protection to all kinds of people. It is Mercury's interest in learning that the Wife of Bath seems to refer to in the prologue to her tale, when she tells about her fifth husband, a young scholar who had been at Oxford:

> Children of Mercury and we of Venus
> Keep up the contrariety between us.

(Nevill Coghill's translation of *Chaucer: The Canterbury Tales*, London, Penguin Books, 1951.)

children's charter, the: education act of 1944 under which the state provided free secondary education for all, the aim being equality of opportunity for every child.

Chinese Gordon: general Charles George Gordon (1833–85), with distinguished military service in China before becoming governor of the Egyptian Sudan and his defence of Khartoum, at which he was killed. He took part in the Chinese war of

1860–2 and suppressed the Taiping rebellion in 1864, was made a mandarin first class but refused presents of money.

chitterlings: frills on a man's shirt front, the rather unpleasant likening of them to the small intestines of animals prepared for food. The nickname began in the late eighteenth century and has almost disappeared, although the fashion has been revived from time to time, including the relaxation of formal evening wear in mid-twentieth century when frilly shirts began to displace the starched front and plain white linen.

chunnel: the projected tunnel under the English channel, the outcome of a plan of many years to link England with France. Work re-started at both ends as a joint British and French venture and progress was made during the nineteen-seventies, but in January, 1975, the British government withdrew its support because of high costs at a time of economic crisis.

city of dreaming spires: felicitous reference to Oxford by Matthew Arnold in *Thyrsis*, 1866—'And that sweet city with her dreaming spires.'

City, the: London's financial centre. 'For some years the City has been arranging finance for Brazil's huge development programme . . .' *The Times* 2 June, 1975. An expression beloved of romantic novelists to explain the occupation of a well-heeled hero is, 'He's something in the City.'

Clapham set: name given by Sydney Smith, wise and witty writer and preacher and one-time canon of St Paul's, London, to a group of men with like political and ethical interests who lived in Clapham at the end of the eighteenth century and the beginning of the nineteenth, prominent among whom was William Wilberforce.

Cleopatra's needle: ancient obelisk on the Thames embankment, London, to which it was brought from Alexandria in 1878. It has nothing to do with Cleopatra, being originally erected at Heliopolis about 1500BC by Thotmes III. It is sixty-eight feet high and weighs 180 tons.

clippie: 'bus conductress, the nickname for women who took over the clipping of tickets from men conductors during the Second World War. It continued as a woman's occupation on many 'bus routes all over the country.

48

Cliveden set, the: politicians, writers and journalists invited to week-end parties at Cliveden, the Buckinghamshire home of Lord and Lady Astor during the nineteen-thirties. Some were alleged to favour appeasement with Nazi Germany. The identification was the invention of Claud Cockburn's satirical political publication, *The Week*.

clunk-click: onomatopoeic name for the fastening of car seat belts, used by the entertainer Jimmy Savile in an official publicity campaign to encourage the use of this safety device, 1974, with the slogan, 'Clunk-click every trip.'

cockers: leather gaiters or knitted woollen leggings, a nickname probably originating from an old English word for a quiver (for arrows), hence a casing for the leg; or there may be a connection with the word 'cocking', meaning the shooting of woodcock, as countrymen going after the birds through scrub would need such protection for their legs.

cock of the north: George, fifth duke of Gordon (1770–1836) who raised the regiment, the Gordon Highlanders, in 1795 and which he commanded in Spain and elsewhere.

cockneys: traditionally those Londoners born within sound of Bow bells (St Mary-le-Bow), Cheapside, distinctive in speech and customs, a nickname used from the seventeenth century. But the word goes further back, to the Latin *coquina*, kitchen, and the cockneys were either 'servants of the kitchen' or addicted to a soft life, hence the old nickname cockney for an effeminate person, pampered by city life. It is allied to the fabled Land of Cockaigne (kitchenland), supposedly filled with sensual delights. A thirteenth-century satire on monks who enjoyed their food and wine at the expense of spiritual devotion tells of them living in this 'land ihote Cokaygne . . . Thogh paradis be miri and bright, Cokaygne is of fairir sight.'

cockpit of Europe: Belgium, wedged between warring nations, scene of so many battles, from Marlborough's victories over the French and Wellington's at Waterloo to the carnage in the First and Second World Wars. Belgium has also been called 'the cross-roads of Europe'.

coffee-table books: those which are left lying around to impress or entertain visitors, usually lavishly illustrated; for idle perusal rather than serious reading from a library shelf, although not necessarily so.

cold war: a state of non-belligerency but ideological conflict between nations—western Europe and the USA in opposition to Russia and the communist eastern block, for example, after 1945. Could Franklyn D. Roosevelt, had he lived longer, asked A. J. P. Taylor in a review of a book about the American president (*The Observer*, 18 May, 1975) have turned the course of events 'away from the Cold War and towards a world truly at peace?'. It was an expression unknown to Ambrose Bierce, but cynics may feel that his whimsical definition of the word 'peace' would be appropriate—'A period of cheating between two periods of fighting.'

cold war witch: Mrs Margaret Thatcher. See *iron lady*.

codpiece: an invention for the embroidered box-like contraption at the front of a fashionable man's breeches in the early part of the sixteenth century, portrayed to perfection in portraits of Henry VIII. The nickname came from the Anglo-Saxon word *cod*, meaning a husk or pod (such as pease-cod) transferred to the scrotum with its testes; the codpiece emphasised the masculine protuberance, and it was used as a convenient receptacle for a handkerchief or sweets, or even as a purse for odd coins. The word cropped up surprisingly as late as 1975 when a writer in *The Observer*, 25 May, praised the 'pop' group The Bay City Rollers: 'They don't quiver their codpieces at the audience like . . .' (mentioning a well-known entertainer).

collop Monday: the day before shrove Tuesday, from the custom in some parts of England of eating collops—slices of meat, often bacon, baked or grilled, sometimes having been coated with egg. The day was also called 'merry Monday'.

colly-molly-puff: a pastry seller, eighteenth century, from the way he cried his wares. He carried cakes in a basket on his head. A letter by Addison in *The Spectator* No 251, 1711, purporting to be a commentary on the street cries of London, refers to the singing call of 'the pastry man, commonly known by the name of the Colly-Molly-Puff'.

common market: convenient name for the European

Economic Community (EEC) formed by the treaty of Rome, 1957. Britain was admitted by signature to the treaty in 1972, membership becoming effective in the following year. Membership which began with six countries was thus enlarged to nine. After much controversy a referendum was arranged for 5 June, 1975—the first ever to be held in Britain—and the public voted more than two to one to stay in the EEC.

congreves: matches, strips of wood coated with chemical which ignited by friction when drawn through a fold of sandpaper, the invention of Sir William Congreve (1772–1828), a military officer who also invented a war rocket and formed rocket companies. See *lucifer, vesta.*

contemptibles (later, old): members of the British expeditionary force who fought in France and Flanders from 1914. They took the name from a sneering remark supposed to have been made by the German emperor ('kaiser Bill') about Britain's 'contemptible little army' and this was given publicity in the papers for propaganda purposes.

corinthians: early nineteenth century dandies, gamblers and well-to-do wastrels, often obstreperous, supporters of pugilism. As well as its reputation for art and sculpture, ancient Corinth was noted for its sophistication and profligacy.

corporal violet: Napoleon Bonaparte who, when defeated by the allied armies in 1814 was allowed to live in exile on the Mediterranean island of Elba, told his followers that he would return to France with the violets. Remembering his former nickname of 'the little corporal' q.v. they changed it to the new one.

cotquean: an effeminate man. No. 482 of *The Spectator*, 1712, contains a letter supposedly written by a wife about the type of man 'who, in several parts of England, goes by the name of "cotquean". I have the misfortune to be joined for life with one of this character, who in reality is more of a woman than I am. He was bred up under the tuition of a tender mother, till she made him as good a housewife as herself . . . He has the whitest hand that you ever saw in your life, and raises paste better than any woman in England. These qualifications make him a sad husband.'

cottonopolis: Manchester, centre of the one-time thriving cotton manufacturing industry which provided Britain's chief export, justifying the slogan 'The nation's bread hangs on Lancashire's thread'. Lancashire's great engineering industry also exported cotton manufacturing machinery, with consequent competition from other countries in world markets. The decline of cotton's importance in the economy took on serious proportions after the Second World War and reached a crisis in the nineteen-seventies. See *king cotton*.

covenanters: Scottish presbyterians who adhered to the National Covenant of 1638 or the Solemn League and Covenant of 1643 to uphold their faith as the religion of the country against attempts to restore the episcopalian church. When the covenants were declared unlawful in 1662 their adherents were persecuted.

cowboy: from the old English name for a lad in charge of cattle on common land. It became almost entirely identified with the men on American western ranches—beloved of fiction and films—until it was shared as a nickname for young city thugs in the mid-twentieth century. Cf. 'cowpuncher'.

cremona: a violin made in the Italian city of Cremona, in the workshops of such masters of the craft as Stradivarius, Amati and Guarnieri. See *strad*.

crookback: Richard III (1452–85), perhaps because of a deformed spine, although contemporary portraits do not show it and he was described as 'comely'. He apparently walked with a stoop.

crouchback: Edmund, earl of Lancaster (and Champagne) (1245–96), second son of Henry III, perhaps for similar reasons as above.

crow's nest: position high on the foremast of a ship to accommodate the look-out man.

crystal palace: an immediate nickname—which became a title—for the edifice of glass and iron designed by Joseph Paxton to accommodate the Great Exhibition of 1851 in Hyde Park, London, later moved to Sydenham and destroyed by fire in 1936. In a poem about the structure, Thackeray called it 'The palace made of windows'.

Cumberland poets: see *Lake poets.*

curse of Scotland, the: nine of diamonds in a pack of cards. There are several theories about the origin. One relates it to the nine lozenges in the coat-of-arms of the Dalrymple family, one of whom was the master (later earl) of Stair who instigated the massacre of Macdonalds by royal troops at Glencoe, 1692.

curthose: in modern words, short-boots or short-socks; Robert II, duke of Normandy (c1054–1134), eldest son of William 'the conqueror', nicknamed thus not so much for his apparel as for the fact that he was a little, stout man—a warrior, nevertheless.

curtmantle: Henry II (1133–89) who introduced a shorter coat or smock from Anjou, of which he was count, perhaps because of his great addiction to hunting. The fashion spread quickly. Alan Lloyd in *King John*, Newton Abbot, David and Charles, 1973, writes of Henry: 'Until the arrival of the new king, English men and women of substance had worn their robes to the ankle, gathered at the waist by a belt or girdle. They also wore an over-mantle of the same length . . . Henry wore his mantle in the style of Anjou, that is, reaching only to the knees.' For excellent descriptions of this remarkable king, first of the plantagenets q.v., see W. L. Warren, *Henry II*, London, Eyre Methuen, 1973.

cutpurse: a thief, from medieval times when leather purses were suspended from the belt by strings. As fashions changed he became a 'pickpocket'. In *Love's Labour's Lost* Berowne speaks of 'pick-purses'. See *Moll cut-purse.*

Cyprians (or Cypriots): early nineteenth century name for high-class prostitutes or courtesans, from the island of Cyprus, legendary home of Aphrodite. These ladies, riding proudly in Hyde Park, London, were also dubbed 'the fashionable impures'.

D

Dad's army: the Local Defence Volunteers (LDV) formed at the outbreak of the Second World War, soon re-named the Home Guard; a posthumous nickname given by those looking back on the exploits of this civilian (though uniformed and attached to army units) force, many of whom were elderly men. A long-running BBC television and radio series under this title established the nickname with affectionate humour.

daisy cutter: in cricket, a ball delivered low before the wicket, shooting into the bat at ground level; in RAF parlance, a good landing, coming down smoothly without bumps.

dancing chancellor, the: Sir Christopher Hatton (1540–91), chancellor of England and favourite of Elizabeth I, noted for his grace and skill in dancing, especially in the galliard which the queen so much enjoyed. 'That Hatton was an accomplished dancer and a skilled performer in the tilt-yard is true enough. But a study of his life dispels the legend that he owed his astonishing progress from an obscure country squire to a dazzling position, with the Woolsack as crowning achievement, to such adventitious graces': Eric St John Brooks, *Sir Christopher Hatton*, London, Cape, 1946.

dandiprat: a small, insignificant person, an urchin, from the sixteenth century; also a small coin. It is difficult to determine which came first, although Ivor Brown, *Chosen Words*, London, Penguin Books, 1961, says 'It began as a small coin and ended as a small boy.' The etymology is obscure: no relationship with 'dandy'.

Darbyites: followers of John Nelson Darby (1800–82), a founder of the Plymouth Brethren q.v. He was a former curate in the Church of England, becoming a much-travelled preacher and a writer of devotional works.

Darby and Joan: an old, happily married couple, originally

54

in poor but contented circumstances. Was there a real Darby and Joan? Legend says there was—living in the West Riding of Yorkshire. *ODEE* traces the term to 1735, a song on the couple being published in that year. Goldsmith uses it in *She Stoops to Conquer*, 1774—'You may be a Darby, but I'll be no Joan.' See *old dutch*.

dark ages, the: a loose definition for a period of intellectual decline after the collapse of classical civilisation, or the fall of the Roman empire, to the renaissance q.v. beginning in the fourteenth century with its revival of learning and humanism; sometimes applied to the period, the fifth to twelfth centuries, for which there is lack of much contemporary records; sometimes only for about three hundred years after 450. The more research is carried out, the shorter and less dark the period appears to be. See *middle ages*.

dark continent, the: Victorian name for Africa, so much of it unexplored. H. M. Stanley wrote *Through the Dark Continent*, 1878, and *In Darkest Africa*, 1890. See *white man's grave*.

dark lady of the sonnets: Shakespeare's beauty whose eyes were 'raven black' in sonnet cxxvii, and whose hair was so coloured in sonnet cxxx—'if hairs be wires, black wires grow on her head'—and to whom several succeeding poems are apparently addressed, and who figures in plays. Her identity has been a guessing game and provided a subject for literary detectives for many years, candidates being numerous. Much has been written about her but that great scholar of the period, A. L. Rowse, *Shakespeare the Man*, London, Macmillan, 1973, is convinced he has discovered who she was.

Davy Jones's locker: sailor's nickname for the sea where drowned men are stowed; probably a corruption of the biblical Jonah who was swallowed by a whale.

D-day: (1) 6 June, 1944, when operation Overlord for the allied invasion of occupied Europe began; (2) 15 February, 1971, the date when decimal currency was introduced in Britain.

dead man's handle: the lever on a diesel or electric train which cuts off power and applies the brakes if the driver releases pressure (in the case of his collapse). This safety device was prominent at the inquiry following London's worst underground train crash, at Moorgate station, in February, 1975, when forty-one people were killed, including the driver.

desert rats: the seventh ~~army~~ [ARMOURED] division serving in north Africa in the Second World War (and later in Europe), adopting the badge of a desert rat, the jerboa.

devil's bones: dice, indicating their temptation to penury, vice, etc.

diamond city: Amsterdam, because of its long reputation for diamond cutting, polishing and marketing, from the seventeenth century.

dicky: a many-purpose nickname—for an ass or donkey, a small bib or apron, a detachable (usually starched) shirt front, a naval officer, a seat at the back of a coach or carriage where a guard or servant sat (and in early motor-cars a similar back seat); also dicky-bird, a small bird or pet name for a bird. The etymology is obscure.

dictionary Johnson: Dr Samuel Johnson (1709–84) because of his *Dictionary of the English Language*, 1755—'and it should not pass unobserved that he has quoted no author whose writings had a tendency to hurt sound religion and morality' says Boswell in his *Life*. He addressed the 'plan' for the dictionary to the earl of Chesterfield ('a nobleman who was very ambitious of literary distinction') and worked three years on it, employing six secretaries. Boswell records that 'the reward of his labour was only fifteen hundred and seventy-five pounds; and when the expense of amanuenses and paper, and other articles, are deducted, his clear profit was very inconsiderable'.

die-hards: those who maintain a theory, argument or conviction in the face of all opposition, stubborn in their beliefs. Also a regimental nickname: see Introduction, p. 8.

diggers: a splinter group from the levellers q.v. during the commonwealth, urging allocation of land for the people, part of the social discontent of the time; an early attempt at land nationalisation.

disc jockey: the presenter of a programme of popular music records on radio, linking the items with commentary. Such 'jockeys' became personalities in their own right from the nineteen-fifties, each with a distinctive style.

dismal science, the: political economy; first used by Carlyle seriously, it became ironically humorous.

dissenters: those religious bodies which dissented from the Church of England, applied from the seventeenth century but superseded by 'nonconformists', the name clinging mainly to the more extreme sects.

distaff day: long-forgotten name for 7 January when women returned to their spinning after the Christmas holiday—to the distaff; usually the work of the unmarried daughters of a family, hence 'spinster'. The female members of a family were known as 'the distaff side'.

dixieland: southern states of the USA, south of the Mason-Dixon line (so called from two Englishmen, Charles Mason and Jeremiah Dixon, who surveyed the boundary between Maryland and Pennsylvania, 1763–7, which was in dispute.) The line separated 'free' from 'slave' states before the civil war, and 'dixieland' became synonymous with the home of the negro. The name was also identified with a style of jazz played in New Orleans from 1910 and which became popular in British theatres and concert halls.

Dizzy: Benjamin Disraeli, first earl of Beaconsfield (1804–81), statesman and novelist, chancellor of the exchequer and prime minister, creator of the conservative party, trusted friend of queen Victoria.

dobbin: farm horse, steady old horse, hence a child's wooden horse. *SOED* dates it back to 1596. Pet name for Robert, as Robin, Bobby.

dockers' k.c., the: Ernest Bevin (1881–1951) who became minister of labour and national service during the Second World War (see 'Bevin boys') and held other high offices. The nickname was given him by the press when he was national organiser of the dockers' union, 1910–21, and in 1920 presented the dockers' demands for better wages and conditions before a commission of inquiry.

57

dogberry, a: an ignorant and officious person, fussing around but not anxious to take much action, as Dogberry the constable in charge of the night watch in Shakespeare's *Much Ado About Nothing*.

Dolly Varden: a youthful style of flowered print dress, slim-waisted, and with flower-bedecked hat worn coquetishly tilted on the head, or a wide-brimmed hat with small crown and tied with ribbon under the chin, as in early illustrations of Dickens's *Barnaby Rudge* where she appears (published 1840) and his description of this simple, gay and pretty girl. The affectionate nickname—'She's a regular Dolly Varden'—was current from mid-Victorian times. Dickens described the locksmith's daughter as a madcap with a roguish face, 'a face lighted up by the loveliest pair of sparkling eyes . . . the face of a pretty, laughing girl; dimpled and fresh, and healthful—the very impersonation of good-humour and blooming beauty'. (Had Gilbert and Sullivan the picture at the back of their minds for the song, 'Take a pair of sparkling eyes'?)

domesday book: popular (unpopular?) nickname given at the time, and becoming established in the language ever since, to the survey of land ownership and tenure, with details of farming and property, carried out by order of William the conqueror, completed 1086, because there could be no appeal against official decisions concerning value and tax. This attempt at a national valuation (and so important an historical record) covered only parts of the country.

Don Giovanni: a handsome and unscrupulous heart-breaker, another name for Don Juan q.v., as in Mozart's opera. Said ensign Spooney in Thackeray's *Vanity Fair*: 'That Osborne's a devil of a fellow . . . and since he's been home they say he's a regular Don Giovanni, by Jove! Stubble and Spooney thought that to be "a regular Don Giovanni, by Jove" was one of the finest qualities a man could possess.'

Don Juan: a great lover, from the legendary character whose ancestry goes further back than his first published appearance in Barcelona, 1630. This dissolute gallant—sometimes with supernatural overtones—has been the subject of books, plays and operas. 'When a man is called a Don Juan, the image projected is of a vastly attractive lady-killer who enters girls' lives and sweeps them off their humdrum sexual course': from an article in *Cosmopolitan*, July, 1974.

doodlebugs: German flying bombs, Hitler's V-1s, aimed at London and other places towards the end of the Second World War; missiles which had a distinctive roar until the motors cut out and the whole craft curved down onto the target; a 'terror' as well as a destructive weapon, like the V-2 rockets that followed. More than ten thousand doodlebugs were launched, each carrying nearly a ton of explosives.

DORA: Defence of the Realm Act, 1914, imposing temporary restrictions. The acronym became a nickname for restrictions of all kinds and was personalised by cartoonists as an elderly woman saying 'no' to most things.

dorcas: a kindly woman, socially-conscious, and one who busies herself in practical charity; from the woman described in *Acts* ix (Tabitha in Aramaic, Dorcas in Greek) whom Peter brought to life when dead. 'She was full of good works and acts of charity ... All the widows stood beside him weeping, and showing tunics and other garments which Dorcas made while she was with them.' Dorcas societies flourished in the churches of the nineteenth and early twentieth centuries, sewing and making garments for the poor.

doubting Thomas: a suspicious person, one hard to convince; from the disciple Thomas ('the twin' q.v.) who refused to believe his companions' story of the resurrection of Jesus until he had seen for himself. The gospel of *John* xx tells how he saw and touched Jesus eight days later.

doughboy: American soldier, from the size and shape of uniform buttons in the civil war, like lumps of dough. Entirely by coincidence the nickname provides a link with the soldier of feudal times whose master paid for his services (or partly) in bread, so that in Anglo-Saxon he would be called *hlafoetan*, loaf-eater; and the Roman fighting servant was *buccellarius*, biscuit-eater. Bread, and dough from which it is made, has a long connection with the soldier. See *GIs*.

drummer: the man who gathers a crowd for his own or someone else's show or sale of wares, as on the fairground or at an open-air market, from the boy who used to play a drum for this purpose to attract attention; also from the drum-beat used by touring recruiting sergeants—'drumming up recruits'. Americans took the word from old English. There are other meanings in slang. Cf. barker, q.v.

dry-bob: boy at Eton who takes up cricket and football, leaving rowing to the wet-bob q.v.

duke, the: Edward Kennedy ('Duke') Ellington (1899–1974), American composer and musician, a leading figure in jazz for half a century. He and his orchestra achieved world fame, as did his own compositions and piano playing at concerts and in recordings. Honorary degrees were conferred on him by several universities.

dundrearies: long side-whiskers sweeping down to the level of the chin, as sported by the British actor Edward A. Sothern (1826–81) in the part of Lord Dundreary in Tom Taylor's comedy *Our American Cousin,* produced in New York, 1858, and in London, 1861. He set a fashion in hairy faces for a short time. Also called 'weepers' and 'Piccadilly weepers'.

E

Early Bird: second of the communication satellites put into orbit, slowed down to the speed of the turning earth, almost hovering in one position over the Atlantic so that television, telephone and telegraphic signals between Europe and America could be relayed at any time, whereas its predecessor —Telstar—had circled the earth, making interchange of transmissions possible only at certain times. Telstar was launched in 1962, Early Bird in 1965.

E-boat alley: the shipping route off the east coast of England during the Second World War, subject to frequent attacks by enemy torpedo-boats.

ebony: *Blackwood's Magazine,* started 1817, or its publisher, William Blackwood (1776–1834), nickname given by James Hogg (the 'Ettrick shepherd', q.v.) who was a contributor.

Edmund ironside: see under *'ironside'*.

Edward's French lady: Julie, mme de St Laurent, with whom prince Edward, duke of Kent (father of queen Victoria), fourth son of George III, was said to have contracted a morganatic marriage. She was his mistress for more than twenty-five years before he married princess Victoria of Leiningen.

Elvis the pelvis: Elvis Presley, internationaly successful 'pop' performer with a long career, from the nineteen-fifties to the 'seventies. The waggling of his hips at concert performances earned him this journalistic tag. He was a vigorous exponent of the rock 'n' roll type of music from 1955.

emerald isle, the: romantic name for Ireland because of its extensive grassland, the richness and contrasts of its shades of green in valleys and on hills.

English Vitruvius, the: Inigo Jones (1573–1652) who introduced the Palladian style of architecture into England. Vitruvius was a Roman architect and engineer, and a treatise on architecture (dedicated to Augustus) had tremendous influence on succeeding generations of builders and designers.

ENSA: one of the many acronyms that have become words, and pronounced as such, standing for Entertainments National Service Association in which actors and actresses, comedians and musicians performed for the forces on war fronts as well as in Britain in the Second World War. There had been a similar organisation in the 1914–18 war.

erk: an aircraftman (AC2), jocularly defined on some wartime airfields as 'the lowest form of animal life'. Partridge claims it as slang, a slurred or shortened pronunciation of air mechanic. See his introduction to *A Dictionary of R.A.F. Slang*, London, Michael Joseph, 1945.

ERNIE: acronym for Electronic Random Number Indicator Equipment, always used (with affection and hope) as a name by people holding premium bonds issued by the department for national savings. ERNIE was designed to select numbers of winning bonds for weekly and monthly prizes in this state lottery.

ESRO: European Space Research Organisation of which

Britain was an active member with nine other countries for the study of the upper atmosphere and cosmic radiation.

eternal city, the: Rome. Byron saluted it as 'The Niobe of nations!' *Childe Harold's Pilgrimage*, iv. The mythological Niobe boasted of her twelve children, so they were slain and she was turned to stone.

Ethelred the unready: Ethelred (or Aethelred) II (c968–1016), king of the English, given the nickname not because he was tardy but because he lacked *rede*, or good counsel, the result being that he had an unhappy reign, following a policy of opportunism, buying off the Danes from time to time and ensuring peace only for short periods.

Eton crop: a boyish hair style for women in the nineteen-twenties.

Ettrick shepherd, the: James Hogg (1770–1835), Scottish poet, born at Ettrick in Selkirkshire, son of a shepherd and tended sheep himself, author of pleasing ballads. Sir Walter Scott gave him powerful encouragement.

Eurocrat: a member of the EEC commission or council of ministers. See *common market*.

EVA: extra vehicular activity, astronauts working outside their spacecraft; the term invented for the American astronauts who did this, the first of them being major E. M. White in 1965 when he left Gemini 4 for twenty minutes while it was in orbit.

F

factory king, the: Richard Oastler (1789–1861), a Yorkshire-man who campaigned against conditions of child labour in the mills, arousing public opinion. He had a leading part in the agitation which produced the ten hours bill and the passing of factory acts. While in the Fleet (q.v.) prison for debt he published the weekly *Fleet Papers* in which factory and poor-law questions were raised.

fair Perdita: Mary Darby Robinson (1758–1800), actress and something of a writer and poet, because of her distinction as Perdita in Shakespeare's *The Winter's Tale* and when she became mistress of the prince of Wales (later prince regent and George IV) who, on seeing her in the part, became her Florizel q.v. (in the play, the prince of Bohemia). They wrote to each other under these names. Subsequently she was mistress of Charles James Fox, but she died in poverty.

familists: their proper name, the Family of Love, a sect founded in Germany in the sixteenth century, spreading to England. Theirs was a simple doctrine of love in religion, for Jesus Christ and for each other in the family of God, although the founder—Hendrik Niclaes (c1502–c1580), a merchant—claimed some kind of divine inspiration.

fancy man: a 'ladies' man', and near slang for a male companion of a married woman, also a ponce. Nickname for a cicisbeo.

fancy, the: of all the 'fancies' (sporting characters) the definite article was particularly associated with the patrons of pugilism, and the nickname extended to the sport itself. Hazlitt, of course, gives the word its correct meaning in his essay *The Fight* in which he describes the contest in 1821 between Bill Neat and Tom Hickman (the 'gas-light man' q.v.): 'Truly, the Fancy are not men of imagination. They judge of what has been, and cannot conceive of anything that is to be ... Besides, there are as many feuds, factions, prejudices, pedantic notions in the Fancy as in the state or in the schools.'

fans: probably a corruption of 'fanciers' (such as pigeon-fanciers), those who devote their time and adulation to a person, entertainment or sport. From 1945 it was adopted as a legitimate word for enthusiastic followers of 'pop' stars and entertainers in general, and of football teams. In the case of football 'fans' the word could be synonymous with 'fanatics', so much trouble caused on the grounds. 'Fans rioted at two football matches yesterday': *The Observer*, 20 April, 1975. Less violent but similarly hysterical fanaticism by 'fans' was frequently reported at 'pop' concerts.

farmer George: George III (1738–1820) one of whose interests outside politics was agriculture. When Arthur Young, writer and pioneer of scientific farming, issued his *Annals of Agriculture*, the King contributed information about his farm at Petersham under the name of Ralph Robinson.

fellow traveller: one who adheres to a system or ideology without necessarily identifying himself publicly with either, applied especially after 1945 to those in sympathy with the communist cause, overtly or under cover.

female Howard, the: Elizabeth Fry (1780–1845), the Quaker prison reformer, because she followed the steps of her predecessor, John Howard (1726–90), a pioneer in this branch of philanthropy. Like Howard, Elizabeth Fry was appalled at prison conditions and she devoted her life to improving them, with special attention to women prisoners. Like Howard, too, she visited prisons abroad as well as in Britain.

few, the: fighter pilots of the RAF at the height of the German air attacks on London and the south-east of England in 1940. Although greatly outnumbered they wreaked havoc on the luftwaffe, with heavy losses to themselves. Paying tribute to these airmen who were 'undaunted by odds, unwearied in their constant challenge and mortal danger', Winston Churchill, prime minister, said in the house of commons, 20 August, 1940: 'Never in the field of human conflict was so much owed by so many to so few'.

field of the cloth of gold: the magnificent display of tents, pavilions and richly caparisoned knights, with lavish entertainment, when Henry VIII had a summit meeting with Francis I of France, near Guines, in June, 1520. No expense was spared for a fortnight, but nothing very much came out of it.

fifth column: traitors or subversive elements in our midst, a designation probably originating in the Spanish Civil War, 1936–9, when the nationalists boasted of a 'fifth column' of sympathisers in besieged Madrid. when 4 columns were of their army were approaching the city.

fifth monarchy men: a puritan sect that came into prominence at the time of Cromwell whose reign they interpreted as

64

heralding the 'fifth monarchy' (following those of Assyria, Persia, Greece and Rome) during which there would be the second coming of Christ. Disappointed, they began to criticise the government and sporadic violence broke out, culminating under Charles II with an attempt to take over London which was easily suppressed and reprisals made. In his *Diary* for January, 1661, Pepys records that on his way to Whitehall he saw two of the leaders 'upon a sledge, who with two more Fifth-Monarchy men were hanged today, and the two first drawn and quartered'. (Typical of the age—and of Pepys—is the sentence immediately following this gruesome entry: 'Went to the theatre . . .')

first gentleman of Europe: George IV, so named by his flatterers. See *Florizel, prinny, Fum the fourth.*

first lady of the air: Gladys Young, distinguished radio actress who died in 1975 after a broadcasting career of nearly forty years. Her first part in a radio play was in 1926: her voice became familiar to millions of listeners. A note in *Radio Times* to a programme in tribute to her said: 'Her contribution to the development of radio drama is incalculable.'

five members, the: John Pym, John Hampden, Denzil Holles, Arthur Hazelrig (or Hesilrige) and William Strode who led the opposition to Charles I in parliament. In January 1642 the king entered the house of commons with soldiers to arrest them, but they were forewarned and were not there. This attempt to impeach the five members was one of the events which led to the outbreak of civil war.

flagellants: (1) various groups of religious extroverts who whipped themselves and each other in public throughout Europe from about 1260, walking in procession through the towns, in punishment for their own and the world's sins. They were much in evidence at times of disaster, such as the 'black death' q.v. Disorders began to occur: there was anti-Jewish incitement and clashes with magistrates and clergy. Eventually they were condemned as heretics. (2) Those members of religious orders who accepted whipping as a discipline and penance, following a long history of flagellation going back to ancient Egypt, Greece and Sparta and the early Christian church.

65

flak: shell-bursts; a compression (and who wouldn't try!) of the German *fliegerabwehrkanone*, anti-aircraft gun.

Flanders mare, the: Henry VIII's unkind nickname for his fourth wife, Anne of Cleves (1515–1557). His dissatisfaction with her resulted in the annulment of their marriage a few months after it was solemnised in 1540.

flapper: the gay young girl of the nineteen-twenties, carefree and flirtatious, although the word was used earlier without being generally accepted. *ODEE* derives the nickname from a young partridge, and *SOED* gives the definition of a young wild duck, applied to girls who have not yet 'put their hair up'. Partridge in *DSUE* admits it as a girl who has neither put up her hair nor yet cut it short according to the fashion of the 'twenties: it flaps in the wind. R. Turner Wilcox in *The Dictionary of Costume*, London, Batsford, 1969, defines the word as such for a girl who has not yet 'come out', and suggests that in America it was used for the girl in short skirts, blouse or sweater who in winter wore galoshes 'which were always unbuckled and flapping'.

In a letter to *The Daily Telegraph*, 25 October, 1975, Miss H. M. Drennan explained the term as she knew it when a girl. 'Her badge of flapperdom, however, was in her hair, which she wore long and tied back with voluminous silk taffeta bows . . . it was these becoming winglike bows which provided the aptness of her title. She had great popularity with bachelors who could tease and mildly flirt without being expected to have matrimonial intentions.' The teenage flapper lost her designation along with her hair when the 'bob' became fashionable in the 'twenties, although the word persisted for some time. She was, at any rate—going back to the original meaning—a 'bird', to use the later slang for her.

flashman: a swell, a patron of pugilism, eighteenth and nineteenth centuries.

Fleet marriages: quiet—or clandestine—weddings carried out by clergymen who were in the Fleet prison, London, for debt; a handy way for them to earn a little money in fees, and for the contracting couple to avoid the expense of an ordinary ceremony—and the attention of their relatives. These secret marriages began around 1613 and continued until 1753 when an act of parliament brought them to an end. On and off it was a profitable racket, both for debtor clergy and tavern keepers nearby who provided rooms and touted for business. This was one of other abuses at the Fleet—founded in Norman times on the bank of the Fleet stream (now a sewer) flowing into the Thames. One was the sale of 'wardenships', the wardens being able to make profits from prisoners, and there was much extortion and cruelty. The prison had a violent history of attack by rioters and destruction by fire—by the 'great fire' q.v. of 1666, and when re-built it was wrecked in the Gordon riots of 1780. Again re-built it resumed its role, mainly as a debtors' prison, until closed in the middle of the nineteenth century.

flicks, the: moving pictures, originating in the USA around 1900 because of the flickering characteristics of the early films, the nickname quickly reaching Britain. It was superseded in America by 'the movies' and in Britain by 'the pictures'. ('We are going to the pictures.')

Florizel: George IV (1762–1830) when prince of Wales, the name he adopted in his affair with Mrs Robinson (see 'fair Perdita'), the actress who attracted his attention in the part of Perdita in Garrick's production of *The Winter's Tale*, 1778. It was a passing, though passionate, episode in his amorous career, not comparable with his later love for Maria Fitzherbert whom he secretly married and whose good influence on him lasted until he became prince regent, despite his selfishness. The prince's several amours and succession of mistresses were public property, and there was little reticence in criticism of him; for example, Pierce Egan's *The Mistress of Royalty, or the loves of Florizel and Perdita.*

flower people (or children): a milder offshoot of the 'hippies' q.v., and like them originating in San Francisco and spreading to England from about 1967. These young people carried flowers in the streets and at concerts, chanting the slogan, 'make love, not war'. They talked of 'flower power'.

flying Finn, the: Paavo Nurmi, famous Finnish runner whose nickname was earned by his successes in the 1924 Olympics.

flying peacemaker, the: journalistic nickname for Henry Alfred Kissinger, secretary of state for USA, because of his tireless journeys by air to various world trouble spots, with special reference to the Israeli-Arab problems in 1975.

flying saucers: or UFOs (unidentified flying objects), appearances in the skies described by observers in various parts of the world as being large and round and travelling at great speed; believed by some to be from far-distant planets, by others to be optical illusions, tricks of light on cloud, meteorological balloons or sheer wishful thinking. Serious investigations were made from the nineteen-fifties. Many sightings could be explained, others could not.

forces' sweetheart, the: Vera Lynn, popular singer who entertained servicemen throughout the Second World War in concerts and on radio. In recognition of her long and distinguished service as an entertainer she was made a dame of the British empire (DBE) June, 1975.

forties, the: see *hungry forties, roaring forties*.

forty-five, the: rising of 1745 when Charles Edward Stuart, the 'young pretender' q.v., backed by Scottish clans, marched south to claim the throne of England and got as far as Derby, within ten days' march of London. Divided counsels and desertions forced him to retreat. He was overwhelmingly defeated at Culloden in April, 1746, and the rebellion crushed. See *bonny prince Charlie, bloody butcher, old pretender*.

forty-niners: those taking part in the 'gold rush' to California, 1849. News of the discovery of rich gold deposits spread in the previous year, and the 'rush' really began in the winter of '48, culminating with as many as eighty thousand men from all parts of America and the world riding and trekking to the plains and foothills. Some made fortunes, most did not. Some perished from thirst, starvation and exposure in 'death valley'. Lawlessness accompanied the frenzy for gold.

forty winks: a doze, short sleep, the explanation (suggesting a few flicks of the eyelids) not as simple as it may seem. Why forty? And is the term not from the middle English *winkis*, meaning sleep? As in the shepherds' play from the Wakefield mysteries: 'We are oft wet and weary when master-men winkis'; that is, when their employers are enjoying the luxury of sleep.

foul-weather Jack: admiral John Byron (1723–86), from his misfortunes at sea. Soon after he joined the navy he was wrecked off the coast of Chile, 1741, and he published an account of his experiences. He commanded the Dolphin on a voyage round the world (1764–6), became governor of Newfoundland and commanded the West Indian fleet.

four-ale bar: the cheaper part of a public house, from the days when beer was fourpence a quart.

four freedoms, the: enunciated by Franklin D. Roosevelt, president of the USA, in a message to congress, 1941, in support of the allies—freedom of speech, freedom of worship, freedom from fear, freedom from want.

free-born John: John Lilburne (c1614–57), a leader of the Levellers, a Christian democratic movement during the civil wars in England and under the commonwealth, its members mainly from the soldiers in the parliamentary army, urging political reforms. Lilburne referred to himself as 'an honest, true-bred, free-born Englishman'. He was high-minded but argumentative: it was said of him that if he were the only person left in the world 'Lilburne would quarrel with John, and John with Lilburne.' He suffered the pillory, imprisonment and fines for his convictions.

free house: public house not tied to a brewery, able to sell a variety of beers.

front bench, the: government ministers (and their parliamentary secretaries); literally the lower benches alongside the table in the centre aisle of the house of commons, below the speaker's chair. The prime minister and his ministers sit on the front bench on the left side of the chamber from the entrance; that is, on the speaker's right as he looks down the aisle. The opposition 'shadow' ministers face them across the table on which there are two despatch boxes. By custom, only ministers and members of the opposition front bench may speak from the despatch boxes. 'When I am speaking from the Despatch Box I am reflecting Government policy as a whole—except when I am clearly reflecting my own policies': Mr Peter Shore, secretary of state for trade in the Labour government, quoted in *The Observer*, 11 May, 1975. See *back bench, the left, shadow cabinet.*

Fum the fourth: George IV (1762–1830), so ridiculed by Byron in *Don Juan* xi:

> Where's Whitbread? Romilly? Where's George the Third?
> Where is his will? (That's not so soon unriddled).
> And where is 'Fum the Fourth', our 'royal bird'?
> Gone down, it seems, to Scotland to be fiddled
> Unto by Sawney's violin, we have heard.

See *first gentleman of Europe, Florizel, prinny.*

fundamentalists: a general term for those Christians who insist on the accuracy of all scriptural writing as divinely inspired, including the 'fundamental' dogmas of the virgin birth, the miracles of Jesus, resurrection of the body, atonement. In the USA fundamentalism became a movement from about 1910, especially in the southern states which H. L. Mencken designated 'the bible belt'. The idea of evolution was contrary to literal acceptance of the bible story of the beginning of the world and human life, so that in 1925 a high school teacher in Dayton, Tennessee, was tried and found guilty of violating state laws by propounding the Darwinian theory, the prosecution being led by William Jennings Bryan. Reports of the trial made headlines in British newspapers.

G

galloping Dick: Richard Ferguson, one of several highwaymen whose exploits earned them nicknames. He was hanged at Aylesbury, 1800. The nickname would have been appropriate for his more famous predecessor, Dick (Richard) Turpin who met a similar fate in 1739, but it does not seem to have been applied.

game chicken, the: Henry (Hen) Pearce, early nineteenth-century pugilist, onetime English champion, pupil of James Belcher whom he defeated at Barnby Moor, near Doncaster, in 1805. Pearce was described in *Boxiana* as 'one of the most heroic and humane champions of England'. He achieved added public fame by the brave rescue of a woman from a burning house.

gamp: borderline slang/nickname for an umbrella, from Mrs Gamp, the nurse in Dickens's *Martin Chuzzlewit*, who always carried one—'a species of gig umbrella—the latter article in colour like a faded leaf, except where a circular patch of a lively blue had been dexterously let in at the top'.

ganymedes: Tudor nickname for a homosexual. In Greek mythology Ganymedes, a handsome youth, was cup-bearer to Zeus. Classical allusions were familiar at court and among the gentry.

gas-man (or gas-light man) the: Tom Hickman, notable pugilist, born in Worcestershire, 1785, winner of many bare-knuckle fights in quick time, and boastful as a result. He is described in *Boxiana* as 'a second Hotspur—impatient—fiery —daring', with the added qualification, 'No boxer ever had a higher opinion of his own powers than Hick. It should seem that he almost flatters himself he is invulnerable.' (Fore-runner of that famous boxer of the nineteen-sixties and 'seventies, Muhammad Ali, who boasted with some justifi-cation, 'I am the greatest!') But Hickman was soundly defeated by Bill Neat, the Bristol butcher, in the contest described by Hazlitt in *The Fight*. (See Introduction, p. 12.) A song of the time begins:

> In eighteen rounds the Gas was spent,
> His pipes lay undefended,
> When Gas-light shares fell cent by cent,
> and thus the battle ended.

Genesis rock: stone brought back from the moon by American astronauts on the Apollo 15 mission, 1971, thought to be more than four billion years old and a clue to the moon's origin.

Geneva bull, the: Stephen Marshall (1594–1655), respected Presbyterian preacher at the time of the commonwealth, noted for his political sermons and support of the bill for abolishing episcopacy. He delivered the funeral service for John Pym. See *five members*.

gentle craft, the: shoemaking, from the patron saints of the craft, Crispin and Crispianus, said to be of noble birth, hence the 'gentle', as in gentleman. The legendary brothers, born in Rome, became Christian missionaries in France and earned their living by making and mending shoes. They were beheaded. Crispin was generally acknowledged as patron saint from the eighth century, his festival being 25 October, the day in 1415 when the battle of Agincourt was fought, which gave the king in *Henry V* a cue for his famous speech:

This day is called the feast of Crispian.
He that outlives this day, and comes home safe,
Will stand a tip-toe when this day is nam'd.

gentleman George: Georges Carpentier (1894–1975), French boxer, heavyweight champion of Europe when he knocked out Joe Beckett in one round in 1919, but in 1921 he was beaten by Jack Dempsey ('the Manassa mauler') in the fourth round for the world heavyweight boxing championship. Carpentier, a debonair fighter, was very popular among the British boxing fraternity.

gentleman in black velvet (or, little gentleman . . .), the: a Jacobite toast to the mole that made the hillock against which William III's horse stumbled, throwing its rider, 1702. The king was already ill, and the shock of the fall (he had a broken collar bone) combined with a chill to cause his death soon afterwards. As he had been invited by the English, with his wife Mary (daughter of James II) to deliver the country from the Stuarts, the Jacobites q.v. had no regrets about his death. They raised their glasses to the mole in his black velvet coat. The toast was later updated to 'the king across the water'.

gentleman Jackson: John Jackson (1769–1845), pugilist, English champion from 1795 to 1803. On retirement he took up a highly successful career as a teacher of boxing.

gentleman Johnny: general John Burgoyne (1722–1792), soldier, member of parliament and dramatist. He is remembered esepcially for the surrender forced upon him by the colonial troops at Saratoga in 1777, a turning-point in the American war of independence. He returned to England amidst public indignation, his honour later restored, and he resumed his career as a witty writer of comedies. Burgoyne was somewhat vain, a bit of a dandy and man-about-town. Horace Walpole called him 'General Swagger'.

gentleman's gentleman: a valet. In fiction, P. G. Wodehouse's Jeeves is the prime example. The term seems to have been first used by Sheridan in *The Rivals*, 1775.

gentlemen of the road: (1) highwaymen. The nickname was used sarcastically in the eighteenth century as the roads became busy with stage coaches as well as horse-riders and family carriages, but stories were told of certain courtesies during robbery—a doffed hat to a lady, a wedding ring spared, a helping hand to the infirm. 'Even a highwayman, in the way of trade, may blow out your brains' writes Hazlitt in *The Fight*, 1822, 'but if he uses foul language at the same time, I should say he was no gentleman.' Sometimes they were called 'knights of the road' or 'Robert's men', from Robin Hood.

(2) tramps have also been nicknamed thus. 'Tramps may be costing the National Health Service millions of pounds by flitting from hospital to hospital ... Gentlemen of the road get first-class accommodation plus medical care, costing up to £100 a week or more': *The Guardian*, 21 April, 1975.

George Cross island: Malta. The medal for gallantry was awarded to the island by George VI, 1942, for the way in which its people had endured attacks by Italian and German aircraft.

Gibson girl: a type of beauty, young and vivacious, vigorous but refined, as portrayed in sketches by the American artist and illustrator, Charles Dana Gibson (1867–1944). These black-and-white drawings, introduced about 1896, achieved tremendous popularity in Britain as well as the USA and were published in book form. The hair style was much copied. His delineations of the 'modern' American girl are said to have been inspired by his wife and her sisters, one of whom was Nancy who became viscountess Astor.

Gideons: international association of business and professional men, founded in 1899 to encourage bible reading, taking their name from Gideon's followers who slew the Midianites (*Judges* vii). There is a wide distribution of bibles, especially to residential hotels for placing in each bedroom.

ginger group: people in any organisation, particularly a political one, whose aim is to stir the others into action.

gippy (or gippo) tummy: forces' nickname for dysentery or diarrhoea, or a general stomach upset, as contracted through service in Egypt. A naval term is 'Malta dog'.

GIs: American servicemen, self-imposed nickname and adopted for them by their allies in the Second World War. Much of the American supplies were marked with these initials, meaning government issue, and the men regarded themselves as such.

gladstone: a light leather travelling bag, named after William Ewart Gladstone (1809–98), prime minister, who carried such, and also a reference to his periods as chancellor of the exchequer. A much shorter-lived nickname of 'gladstone' was given to cheap French wines because in 1860, during his chancellorship, he reduced the duty on them.

Glasites: see *Sandemanians*.

Gloriana: one of the many adulatory names for Elizabeth I, bestowed on her by Edmund Spenser (c1552–99) in his long allegory *The Faerie Queene*. When he published the first three books of the work in 1590 he addressed an introduction to Sir Walter Raleigh in which he said: 'In that Faerie Queene I meane glory in my general intention, but in my particular I conceive the most excellent and glorious person of our soveraine the Queene, and her kingdom in Faery land.'

glorious revolution, the: events of 1688 when James II fled to France and William of Orange and his wife Mary, James's daughter, accepted the invitation to share the throne of England. See *orangemen*.

G-man: government man, an agent of the US federal bureau of investigation.

gnomes of Zurich: Swiss bankers and financiers, the nickname given by newspaper 'city page' writers from the nineteen-sixties. The Labour peer, Lord George Brown, was one of the first politicians to use the term which 'became so embedded in our language that we would have senior Swiss bankers appearing on the television and saying: "Well, I am, how you say, a gnome?" ' (*The Guardian*, 19 May, 1975).

goddams: the English as the French nicknamed them because of the expletive they commonly used, the slurred 'God damn

74

it!' The word has a long history, going back to the fifteenth century, but it was revived, with the popularity of the 'grand tour' q.v. in the eighteenth. See *muscadins*. (Another example of compression is 'godden', obsolete word for 'good evening'.)

God's acre: a churchyard.

God's Sunday: Easter Sunday.

Goldy: Dr Johnson's nickname for Oliver Goldsmith (1728–74). Horace Walpole called him 'the inspired idiot'. See also *Noll.*

good book, the: the bible.

goose step: German style of military marching because it looks like that, legs moving from the hips and swinging high without bending the knees; introduced into the Prussian army under Frederick 'the great' (1712–86). Other armies, notably the Russian, introduced a similar step.

gov'nor, the: (1) Francis Albert (Frank) Sinatra (b1915), American singer and actor, formerly a member of Tommy Dorsey's orchestra, for long a most popular entertainer. (2) George Edwardes (1852–1915), British theatrical manager and impressario, who for nearly thirty years was manager of the Gaiety theatre, London: he produced many successful musical plays. (Several other 'showbiz' people have been thus named.)

grand old man, the: William Ewart Gladstone (1809–98) towards the end of his life when he had become as established an elder statesman as Victoria had a queen, and especially during the few years of his retirement after 1894. His long political career began in 1833 and his high offices included the premiership four times. See *old glad-eye.*

grand tour: the fashion for sending scions of noble and wealthy families, often accompanied by their tutors, around Europe to enhance their education and knowledge of the world, beginning in the seventeenth century with visits to France, Holland and Germany, and extending to Switzerland, Italy and other parts. Typical of the early excursionists was William

Penn whose father, the admiral, packed him off in the hope of getting his interest in Quakerism out of his system (see Pepys's *Diary*, August, 1664). The heyday of the grand tour was the eighteenth century when *milords Anglais*, with tutors nicknamed 'bear leaders', were regarded as the big spenders to be flattered, impressed and often fleeced. Such a tour lasted months or one or two years. Of the many diaries kept, John Evelyn's gives one of the best first-hand accounts of a long seventeenth century tour, and for later adventures see Laurence Sterne's *A Sentimental Journey*, 1768.

grass roots: the general, unsung population, the ordinary voters whose opinions are supposed to be revered by politicians who grow from them and are sustained by them; a term popularised from the nineteen-sixties.

grass widow: *SOED* gives an early meaning as an unmarried woman who has cohabited with a man, going back to 1528. The nickname, or colloquialism, has had other interpretations, such as a divorced woman or a discarded mistress; but it has been modernised as a reference to a wife whose husband is temporarily absent for legitimate reasons, on business, for example, or for a sporting pursuit (the latter condition often specified as 'golfing widow', 'angling widow', etc.). There is a rural link with a working horse 'put out to grass', resting or retired to the pastures. With many wives going out to work or enlarging their interests outside the home, from mid-twentieth century, a male counterpart of 'grass widower' has been established.

great Cham (of literature), the: Dr Samuel Johnson (1709–84), thus dubbed by his contemporary, Tobias George Smollett. Other names for the learned gentleman were 'the great moralist', 'the English Socrates', and 'Ursa Major', bestowed by Boswell's father and used by C. E. Vulliamy as the title of a witty biography.

great commoner, the: (1) William Pitt the elder, first earl of Chatham (1708–78); (2) also applied to W. E. Gladstone because he declined a peerage. See *grand old man*.

great fire (of London): the fire which began in Pudding lane, 2 September, 1666, and fanned by a strong easterly wind swept through the wood and plaster-and-lath houses, destroying a large part of the city down to the Thames, including St Paul's. For eye-witness accounts see the *Diaries* of Pepys and Evelyn. Following closely on the 'great plague' q.v. the fire had healthy results, and re-planning of the city and rebuilding in brick and stone laid the foundations of modern London. History may use the term for the much greater conflagrations, 1940–44: see *blitz*.

great Paul: the bell in St Paul's cathedral, London, weighing over seventeen tons, nearly nine feet high, hung in 1882.

great plague, the: the epidemic of bubonic fever (known in the fourteenth century as the 'black death' q.v.) which ravaged London, reaching its height in 1665, and spreading to other places. The death toll was enormous: an estimate of seventy thousand has been given. The disease was carried by rats and fleas. As well as public records there are several contemporary accounts, including Pepys's and Evelyn's *Diaries*. See *plague Sunday*.

great rebellion, the: generic term for the civil wars (1642–52), beginning with the raising of Charles I's standard at Nottingham. The country's loyalties were divided between royalists and parliamentarians. The 'rebellion' is usually divided into two wars, the first 1642–6, the second 1648–52.

great train robbery, the: spectacular hold-up of a Glasgow-to-London train in Buckinghamshire, 1963, when two-and-a-half million pounds were stolen from the mail van, described as 'the crime of the century' and with which other robberies were compared. The police made quick arrests, but investigations persisted for ten years to trace the last of the gang. Newspaper headlines for the long-running story were inspired by the title of an early silent film classic, *The Great Train Robbery*, known as 'grandfather of American westerns'.

great unknown, the: Sir Walter Scott (1771–1832) whose novels for ten years were published anonymously, credited as 'by the author of *Waverley*', the first of a long series, 1814. He had gone into partnership with James Ballantyne, printer, and they hid the identity of authorship.

great unwashed, the: working-class people, the 'lower

orders', a nickname used by Edmund Burke (1729–97), probably remembering Shakespeare's reference to 'Another lean unwash'd artificer', *King John* (IV, ii).

great wen, the: London, so dubbed by William Cobbett (1762–1835) in *Rural Rides*, disliking the sprawling city. See *smoke*.

green-eyed monster, the: jealousy. Iago in *Othello* says: 'O! beware, my lord, of jealousy; it is the green-eyed monster which doth mock the meat it feeds on.' (III, iii.)

green pound: an invention of 1975 to describe an accounting device within the 'common market' q.v. for calculating British farm prices. 'The scheme, approved by ministers of agriculture of the Nine, involves a devaluation of the so-called "green pound" by 5 per cent . . .': *The Times*, 23 July, 1975, reporting a plan to give aid to British farmers. See *snake*.

green ribbon men (or green ribbon club): seventeenth century political opponents of the court, the early whigs q.v. who met in taverns and coffee houses and wore a bow of green ribbon in their hats for identification. They were mainly associated with the King's Head tavern at the corner of Fleet Street and Chancery Lane, London, from about 1675, and here the news was discussed and plots hatched. It became an operational headquarters for the whig faction, and many prominent men were members of the club. (Green was a colour of opposition from Cromwellian days. See under *reds*.)

green room: the backstage retiring or waiting room for actors, originally decorated green as restful to the eyes, in those theatres which were fortunate to have such a facility. Privileged visitors were admitted.

greenshirts: supporters of a social credit system propounded by major C. H. Douglas, an economist, who from the nineteen-twenties argued for a periodic valuation of British output and a national dividend distribution. His more enthusiastic followers adopted a green shirt.

gregorian: a wig, fashionable in the latter part of Elizabeth I's reign, named after a barber called Gregory whose shop was in the Strand, London.

gremlins: mischievous spirits held accountable for inexplicable mishaps or trouble in general. Folklore goblins were thus enrolled into RAF language in the Second World War. (In my own experience we had a love-hate relationship with gremlins in the RAF—'The gremlins have got into it', 'We couldn't beat the gremlins'—and they accompanied most crews. V.N.)

groaner, the (or old groaner): Harry Lillis 'Bing' Crosby, American singer and film actor, formerly vocalist with Paul Whiteman's orchestra, internationally famous through his recordings, a pioneer 'crooner'. He appeared in more than fifty films.

grocer, the: Edward R. G. Heath before he became prime minister, the sarcastic nickname arising from his early negotiations for Britain's entry into the common market q.v.; popularised in the satirical publication *Private Eye*. Similarly, Mrs Margaret Thatcher, who succeeded him as leader of the Conservative party, was nicknamed 'the grocer's daughter'.

grog: rum diluted with water, as introduced by admiral Edward Vernon (1684–1757) in 1740: his nickname was 'old grog' because of his addiction to a grogram cloak—a coarse material of silk and wool. The nickname was also given by sailors to public houses ashore—'grog shop', a place where spirits were sold.

groundlings: spectators in the Elizabethan theatre who stood on the ground around the stage because they could not afford seats in the galleries. (A few privileged people sat on the stage itself.) Hence the extended meaning for the poorer section of the public. Public playhouses, circular or octagonal in shape (although the Fortune, built later, was square) had a stage in the middle of an open space with a roofed section at the back of it. The 'groundlings' crowded at the front and sides. In his instructions to the players who have come to the castle, Hamlet says: 'O! it offends me to the soul to hear a robustious periwig-pated fellow tear a passion to tatters, in very rage, to split the ears of the groundlings . . .': *Hamlet* (III, ii).

growlers: four-wheeled horse-drawn cabs which plied for hire in the latter part of the nineteenth century and the early twentieth, because of the sound they made on cobblestone and wooden blocks. Some people applied the nickname to the drivers whose moroseness was in contrast with drivers of the more sprightly hansom q.v.

Grub street: an actual street in the Cripplegate area of London, it became the nickname for aspiring or hack writers because many of them lived there cheaply in the late seventeenth and eighteenth centuries, willing to turn their talents in any direction that was profitable, from translations to political pamphlets, scurrilous broadsheets and bawdy verse; extended to mean poor and struggling authors generally and the kind of work they undertook. Dr Johnson made a facetious remark about himself when in his *Dictionary* he defined the words as 'the name of a street in London, much inhabited by writers of small histories, dictionaries and temporary poems; whence any mean production is called Grub-street'. Cf. his definition of lexicographer: 'a writer of dictionaries, a harmless drudge'.

gun that won the west: the American Winchester rifle, introduced in 1856, one of the earliest magazine rifles, used with great effect against the Indians when opening-up new territories; familiar to British cinema-goers through all the cowboy-and-Indian films.

H

Hadrian's wall: convenient name for the fortification, seventy-three miles long, between the Solway Firth and Wallsend-on-Tyne, first constructed as a rampart with a ditch in front and a road behind about 122 to defend the northern frontier of the Roman province of Britain at the command of emperor Hadrian on one of his many journeys throughout his empire. It was originally mainly a turf wall, rebuilt in stone by Septimus Severus about 208, with forts and blockhouses along its length.

hair shirt budget: the severe budget introduced by the Labour chancellor of the exchequer, Denis Healey, April, 1975, in which beer and cigarettes were raised in price, income tax increased, car tax doubled (at a time when so many 'workers' could now afford cars after continuing wage increases, keeping pace with or exceeding inflation), heavy duties on whisky and wines, phasing-out of subsidies, and the accent on austerity and wage restraint.

hammer of the Scots: Edward I (1239–1307), although he was just as severe in his campaign against the Welsh; a great administrator as well as warrior. The plain slab under which he was buried in Westminster abbey bore the inscription *Edwardus primus Scottorum malleus hic est.* Also called 'longshanks' q.v.

hanging judge, the: John Toler (1745–1831), chief justice of the common pleas in Ireland, noted for his harsh treatment of rebels with whom he joked when passing sentence of death. He had a coarse sense of humour and a cruel streak, and according to *DNB* 'showed gross partiality, buffoonery, and scant legal knowledge on the bench'.

hansom: light cab invented by the Yorkshire architect J. A. Hansom, 1834, originally with a low-slung carriage between two large wheels and the driver's seat at the side; improved to place the driver at the back, with double doors in front, giving him a clear view and the passengers (maximum two) cosily placed behind the horse. It was a favourite hired vehicle throughout Victorian and into Edwardian times. Writing of his boyhood at the end of the nineteenth century, Guy Chapman *A Kind of Survivor*, London, Gollancz, 1975, says: 'Yet the town at night was quiet enough, except for whistles blown for cabs: one for a hansom, two for a four-wheeler, a quiet gently broken by the sweetest of all London sounds, the sedate clip-clop of a horse's hoofs on the wood blocks.'

hardware: units making up a computer system. See *software.* Also euphemism for tanks, guns and other military weapons, current in the nineteen-sixties and seventies.

harefoot: Harold I, illegitimate son of Canute whom he briefly succeeded as king of England in opposition to his legitimate brother, Hardicanute, whose mother—queen Emma —was banished from the kingdom. He died in 1040. The nickname-surname by which he was known was probably given because of his speed in action; or there could have been a deformity.

havelock: a light (usually white) covering for a soldier's cap, with a flap to cover the back of the neck as protection against sunstroke, first worn by troops under the command of Sir Henry Havelock (1795–1857), the distinguished officer in Afghanistan and India, and whose column relieved Lucknow in the Indian mutiny.

haves and have-nots: description current from the nineteen-fifties for the nations with a high standard of living compared with those where poverty was widespread, subjected to floods and famine and with undeveloped resources. Karl Marx (1818–83) used the term long before that, but as applicable to sections of the community that 'have' possessions, comfort and wealth and the larger masses that 'have not', resulting in a class struggle. Benjamin Disraeli (Lord Beaconsfield) drew striking attention to these sections of society—'the two nations' as he called them—in his novel *Sybil*, 1845, discussing the relationship between rich and poor.

hawkubites: see *mohocks*.

heart of Midlothian: the old jail in Edinburgh, capital of the county of Midlothian, demolished in 1817. Walter Scott used it as the title to one of his novels.

Hereward the wake: heroic resistance fighter against the Norman conquerors of England, always watchful and alert against their incursions into his domain in the Lincolnshire fens. His exploits became legendary, and the nickname was awarded long after his death around the end of the eleventh century, as was another tribute, 'England's darling'. (Alfred 'the great' was also given the honorific, 'England's darling'.)

herring pond, the: the Atlantic ocean, because of the vast shoals of herring around the northern shores on both sides.

highbrow: an intellectual, or one considered to be such by those less endowed with mental ability; nickname variation of the slang 'egg-head' which is more derisive, suggesting that a 'highbrow' is similar to an 'egg-head' except that the former has a higher quality of brain content within the cranium. All of it based on the belief that the higher the forehead the greater the intelligence. See *lowbrow*.

Highland laddie, the: Scots' affectionate nickname for prince Charles Edward Stuart, 'bonnie prince Charlie', the 'young pretender' q.v.

hippies: young men and women who rejected convention in dress and behaviour, professing disillusion with conditions and accepted social aims, taking to drugs: the 'drop outs' of the nineteen-sixties and on, successors to 'beatniks' q.v. but usually less violent, with a greater tendency to wander the country and the world, in groups and pairs, playing guitars, aimlessly or joining with mystic cults. They were often in trouble with the authorities as squatters, vagabonds, drug-takers. The word may come from 'hip', meaning depressed, suggesting melancholia, an old shortening of 'hypochondria'.

hob: a variant of Rob, short for Robin, meaning a rustic as well as an elf or sprite. Cf. Jacques Bonhomme, nickname for a French peasant. Cf. also *hodge* q.v.

hobble skirts: one of the more ridiculous of women's fashions, skirts narrowed above the ankles so that their wearers took short, unsteady steps; in fact, 'hobbled'. They were a cartoonist's delight. In July, 1911, a *Punch* cartoon showed two women hopping, one of them saying: 'Hurry up, Mabel; you'll never catch the train if you keep on trying to run.'

hocktide: part of the Easter festival, originating in medieval England when the second Monday and Tuesday after Easter Sunday were given over to boisterous play. The custom in many villages was for women on hock Monday to capture and tie the men, and to release them on payment of a fine: on the following day it was the men's turn. Money raised was given to the church. There was a tradition that the custom commemorated victory over the Danes (or was it buying them off? See *'Ethelred the unready'*). The etymology of 'hock' is doubtful, but it provided a new word in the language—to pawn, as Ethelred did his country.

hocus pocus: Elizabethan nickname for a conjuror or magician, extended to mean an imposter, trickery and non-sense. Such gentry bedazzled the fairground crowds with a mock-Latin incantation, including these words, as cards and other things appeared and disappeared by sleight of hand.

hodge: a yokel, simple countryman, short for Roger; probably derived from the servant in William Stevenson's play, *Gammer Gurton's Needle*, 1575. Cf. *hob* (above).

holy club: one of the nicknames given by Oxford under-graduates in 1729 to the group of young men associated with John and Charles Wesley and John Whitefield who met to study the scriptures, out of which grew the 'methodists', q.v.

holy maid of Kent: see *nun of Kent*.

holy week: the week in the Christian calendar immediately preceding Easter Sunday, the earliest references to the special observances at this time dating to the latter part of the third century.

homburg: a soft felt hat as made at Homburg-vor-der-Höhe in Germany, popularised by Edward VII who 'took the waters' there at the chalybeate springs. Its reputation as a spa began in 1834 and when casinos were set up to attract visitors it became one of the most fashionable health-resorts in Europe.

home counties: the seven counties around London—Middle-sex, Surrey, Kent, Essex, Hertfordshire, Buckinghamshire, Berkshire.

hooverers: nickname invented for fishermen and their vessels using large nets to take up gigantic catches, then suctioning the contents in the manner of a vacuum cleaner of that brand name, a technique that threatened European herring shoals in the nineteen-seventies. 'Hoovering is a term used by fisher-men to describe the process of sweeping the sea with massive nets and then using suction to deposit the entire contents of whatever size and type into the hold to be turned into fishy pulp': *The Observer*, 6 April, 1975.

horseless carriage: nickname for the early motor-car which was adopted for a short time as a proper name, so much so that a firm was established called The Great Horseless Carriage Co., Ltd. An advertisement by this firm in 1896, addressed 'to the nobility and gentry', extolled the merits of the Daimler wagonette, with an illustration of the twin-cylinder six h.p. car which had a long-handle steering device and could seat three people as well as the driver. 'This novel vehicle', said the advertisement, 'is propelled by an internal combustion engine . . . The mechanical carriage will attain the comfortable speed of twelve miles per hour on the level, while hills can be ascended and descended in safety.'

hot gospeller: a fervent evangelist; old nickname for a puritan preacher of hell-fire for sinners.

Hotspur: Henry Percy (1364–1403), eldest son of the first earl of Northumberland, the nickname awarded when he was twenty because of his tireless and vigorous skirmishing along the Scottish border. From boyhood, Harry Hotspur was a fearless fighter and his valour in many battles became legendary: he was idolised by soldiers, esquires and knights—tall, handsome with black curling hair, but moody and with a hesitant or thickness of speech. Shakespeare stresses his virtue and prowess in I *King Henry IV*.

house, the: houses of parliament, more commonly the house of commons. Dickens, who as a young man was a reporter there, has Twemlow in *Our Mutual Friend* (1865) saying 'it is the best club in London'. The nickname has also been given to the London stock exchange.

huguenots: nickname for French protestants from the sixteenth century, one theory being that it was derived from the gate of king Hugo at Tours near which followers of Luther used to meet at night, and a monk so called them in a sermon. It may have coincided neatly with an old French word for a small pot. As with 'quakers' q.v., a term of derision was honorably adopted and became familiar in England when many of them crossed the channel to escape persecution from about 1685.

hungry forties: the period of the eighteen-forties just before the repeal of the corn laws (which did not come into effect until 1849) and the cost of bread had risen beyond the means of poorer people, because of duties on imported corn to keep up the price of native cereals, despite great efforts by the free trade movement. While in Ireland the potato crop, on which the majority of people depended, failed and there was widespread famine, 1845–7. Public and private relief work was undertaken, but it was estimated that more than two hundred thousand people died of starvation, or fever enhanced by shortage of food, and there was mass emigration from Ireland.

Huntingdonians: a sect of methodists, known more precisely as Lady Huntingdon's connection, after Selina, widow of the ninth earl of Huntingdon, who devoted herself to evangelical religion, aided by her chaplain, George Whitefield, from 1748. His Calvinism led to a break with the Wesleyan methodists amd he and the countess thought alike. She opened a training college for ministers and built chapels in Bath, Brighton, London, Tunbridge Wells and elsewhere. Eventually there was an amalgamation with congregationalists. See *holy club*, *methodists*.

hydrospace: the seas, a convenient word which came into use in the late nineteen-sixties when the study of underwater resources and pollution was intensified, in contradistinction with 'outerspace' and its exploration.

I

immortal tinker, the: John Bunyan (1628–88) who worked at his father's trade as a tinker before becoming a soldier on the parliamentary side and then turning to preaching and writing. It was probably during his second imprisonment that he began his famous *The Pilgrim's Progress*. Another honorific is 'the immortal dreamer'.

imperial: a pointed tuft of hair on a man's chin, as worn (with moustache) by Napoleon III (1808–73), emperor of the French. He spent much time in London, and returned to England after the Franco-Prussian war.

indian summer: (1) originally an American term for a period of warm sunny weather in the fall, adopted in Britain for a similar spell of imprecise date, taking over from what had been known as St Martin's summer which strictly fell between St Luke's day (18 October) and St Martin's day (11 November). (2) Extended to denote the period in middle age or later when those who are fortunate enough to enjoy a resurgence of youth, success in undertakings, or just blissful tranquillity. It is a most convenient term because it can also apply to public affairs or epochs in history.

inexpressibles: men's trousers, probably the invention of John Wolcot (1738–1819), a doctor who wrote under the name of Peter Pindar (after the ancient Greek poet) and who described the prince regent's elegant breeches in this way. Another euphemism was 'indescribables'. Cf. *unmentionables* q.v.

Inghamites: followers of Benjamin Ingham (1713–72), noted religious leader, a staunch methodist at Oxford and who accompanied the Wesleys to Georgia; then he joined the Moravians and later the Sandemanians (both q.v.).

iron chancellor, the: prince Otto E. L. Bismarck (1815–98), Prussian stateman and a founder of the German empire of which he became first chancellor, named because of his inflexible character and his remark about his policy being founded on 'blood and iron'. He used the words in a speech to the Prussian parliament in 1862, referring to Prussia's boundaries.

ironclad: nineteenth-century name for wooden warships which had the hull above water plated with iron.

iron curtain: the ideological boundary between the so-called 'free world' and the communist-dominated countries, the designation current from the end of the Second World War when, in March, 1946, Winston Churchill made a speech in which he said, 'From Stettin in the Baltic to Trieste in the Adriatic an iron curtain has descended across the continent.' The 'iron curtain countries' came to mean those on the eastern side, Russia and the communist bloc.

iron duke, the: the first duke of Wellington (1769–1852), great soldier and statesman, inflexible as was the 'iron

87

chancellor' (above) in battle and politics. The nickname was used when he put up iron shutters (and two cannon in the gateway) at his home, Apsley House, London, during riots in favour of the reform bill. Several iron statues were erected in his memory.

iron horse: the early steam locomotive. The railway tracks were dubbed 'the iron road'.

iron lady (of British politics): nickname given to Mrs Margaret Thatcher, leader of the Conservative party in opposition, by the Russian paper *Red Star* because of her speeches attacking the Russian arms programme and the danger of Communist aggression, January, 1976. In the following month she was referred to in Moscow as 'the Cold War Witch'.

ironside: Edmund (or Eadmund), son of Ethelred 'the unready' q.v., because he was a valiant fighter and noted for his great strength. Edmund (c980–1016), king of the West Saxons, fought against the Danes until a division of the kingdom was agreed upon, Canute ruling the north, Edmund the south.

ironsides: cavalrymen under Oliver Cromwell at the start of the civil wars, nicknamed thus respectfully by prince Rupert commanding horsemen on the other side, because of their strict discipline as well as their armour. Rupert also called Cromwell himself 'old ironsides', and later the nickname was applied to the parliamentary forces generally.

iron maiden (or virgin): one of the many diabolical instruments of torture devised from the middle ages on, this one a kind of wooden coffin shaped like a figure and with iron spikes embedded in it, into which a prisoner was squeezed.

'It' girl, the: Clara Bow (1905–1965), popular actress of the silent films, personifying the 'flapper' q.v. attractions of the nineteen-twenties, gay and pretty, kissable cupid's bow lips, short hair, innocently challenging eyes, wearing beads and bangles. 'It' became the indefinable something that epitomised feminine appeal, as Kipling long before had used it in a short story, and Elinor Glyn in *It and Other Stories*: in short, sex appeal.

ITMA: acronym-into-word for the long-running radio comedy series from 1939 until the death of Tommy Handley, its leading figure, in 1949. The initials, standing for 'It's That Man Again', were on everyone's lips during the war, as were the many catch phrases introduced by the team, sustaining morale by laughing at Hitler and all the discomforts and restrictions of wartime.

J

Jack: one of the most obliging nicknames in the language, with a multiplicity of uses, emerging in many cases to the honour of a proper name; the diminutive of John or James (Jacobus). It was so familiar a name that it was used for the ordinary working man, 'every man jack' and 'jack of all trades'. We meet him in Jack Frost (personification of winter), Jack-a-Lent (a figure to throw balls and stones at in Lenten games), Jack-in-the-green (usually a chimney sweep covered with leaves on May Day); and he pops up in jack-in-the-box, and rises above his station when he becomes a jack-in-office. As befitted his lowly status, Jack was also something small, like jacksprat (a dwarf), and the name was given to the target wood rolled out first in a game of bowls; and he could be used in the nickname for an impudent fellow or coxcomb, coupled with that of a cheeky monkey, jackanapes—'I will teach a scurvy jack-a-nape priest to meddle or make', says Caius in *The Merry Wives of Windsor* (I, iv). Jack is also a small flag on the jack-staff at the bow of a ship, indicating nationality, or Union Jack, bringing us back to king James, or Jacobus.

A 'jack' in medieval times was a waxed leather tankard, and also the quilted leather coat, often plated with metal, worn by the ordinary foot soldier, the latter having its own diminutive of our present-day jacket. See *union jack*.

jack-a-dandy: a man who fancies himself and his appearance, a fop.

jack o' lantern: a night watchman who carried such illumination.

jack tar: a sailor, from the eighteenth century, because of the tar used for caulking the seams of ships (used with oakum) and the tarred canvas breeches he wore.

Jack the ripper: popular nickname for the unknown murderer of eight prostitutes in the east end of London, 1887–9, their mutilated bodies suggesting he might be a sex-maniac butcher, one of the many theories about his identity, including that of a sailor or even a titled person. The case has been the subject of much investigation and speculation since then. A note found was probably a hoax:

> I'm not a butcher,
> Nor a Yid,
> Nor yet a foreign skipper,
> But I'm your own light-hearted friend,
> Yours truly, Jack the Ripper.

Jacobites: supporters of the house of Stuart for succession to the British throne, in the persons of James II and his descendants. They became active after James fled to France in 1688, and their efforts led to the risings of 1715 and 1745. See *forty-five; old* and *young pretender*.

jacobus: a gold coin struck in the reign of James I.

James the white: James Butler, twelfth earl and first duke of Ormonde in the Irish peerage, commander of the royalist forces in Ireland against the parliamentary army under Cromwell, because of his long fair hair. Portraits show his hair to be luxuriously sweeping well below his shoulders. He was lord lieutenant of Ireland and lord high steward at the coronations of Charles II and James II.

Jarrow crusade: the march of unemployed men from Jarrow, county Durham, to London, 1936, to draw attention to great hardships in the town due to mass unemployment. Jarrow, largely dependent on shipbuilding, became almost derelict during the depression of the 'thirties. The long march aroused tremendous sympathy and stimulated pressure on parliament. (Jarrow's plight was part of what was known as 'the great slump' when unemployment throughout the country reached a peak of nearly three million in the 1932–3 winter.)

jarvey: nickname for a hackney-coach driver and also used for the vehicle itself in the nineteenth century; from the personal name Jarvis or Jervis. *ODEE* suggests an allusion to St Gervase whose emblem is a whip: he was beaten to death.

Jemmy Twitcher: John Montagu, fourth earl of Sandwich (1718–92), an extremely unpopular man, partly because of widespread corruption in the navy when he was first lord of the admiralty, partly because he turned against his friend John Wilkes and took a leading part in prosecuting him, the latter behaviour earning him the nickname from the *Beggar's Opera*. A publication, the *Life, Adventures, Intrigues and Amours of the celebrated Jemmy Twitcher*, 1770, was libellous. Sandwich was a hell-fire rake in his youth. Nevertheless, his name has gone into history because captain Cook named the Sandwich islands after him, and he is remembered for a way of eating meat between two slices of bread. See *monks of Medmenham Abbey* and *sandwich*.

jerry: more correctly, gerry, but British soldiers used the spelling as a nickname for Germans: in the Second World War it was transferred by the RAF and Observer Corps to an enemy aircraft—'It's a jerry.'

jerry-can: petrol or water container designed by the Germans and introduced in north Africa in the Second World War.

Jersey lily, the: Lily Langtry (1852–1929), beautiful actress, born in Jersey, daughter of a dean, who made her London debut in *She Stoops to Conquer*, 1881. She became an intimate friend of Edward VII when prince of Wales.

jewel of the Adriatic: Venice, so popular with British tourists from the eighteenth century, one of many honorifics. For more detail see *bride of the sea*.

Jezebel: a high-spirited, even vicious woman, especially one who paints her face to lure men, as Jezebel whom Ahab married, and who 'When Jehu came to Jezreel . . . she painted her eyes, and adorned her head, and looked out of the window' (2 *Kings*, ix). A mock letter in *The Spectator*, No 175 1711, is from a studious bachelor complaining of the distraction by a woman living in lodgings opposite to him: 'You are to know, Sir, that a Jezebel (so called by the neighbourhood from displaying her pernicious charms at her window) appears constantly dressed at her sash, and has a thousand little tricks and fooleries to attract the eyes of all the idle young fellows . . .' See *picts*.

Jezreelites: followers of James White (1840–85), former soldier who took the names of James Jershom Jezreel and founded a religious sect in 1875 whose aim was to be numbered among the elect on the day of judgment, 'sealed' on the forehead as were the hundred and forty-four thousand in *Revelation* vii. He called his wife queen Esther.

Jix: William Joynson-Hicks, first viscount Brentford (1865–1932), politician who held several high offices, including those of postmaster-general, financial secretary to the treasury, minister of health and home secretary. He was also interested in air and military affairs.

joe (or Joe Miller): at first, a joke; then a worn-out joke, a 'chestnut', from long usage; named after Joe Miller (1684–1738), a popular comedian. A jest-book of stories credited to him was brought out in 1739.

joe (or joey): (1) a small silver coin, worth fourpence, current from 1836, useful for paying cab fares; transferred for a time to the silver 'threepenny bit'. (2) Joey with a capital letter was a nickname for Joseph Chamberlain (1836–1914) and for his radical followers.

jockey of Norfolk: John Howard, first duke of Norfolk (c1430–85), distinguished soldier on the Yorkist side and in France, created duke and earl marshal by Richard III to whose allegiance he had turned. He was killed at Bosworth. He is referred to by this nickname in *King Richard III* (V, iii) when a mocking verse is sent to him on the battlefield, beginning, 'Jockey of Norfolk be not too bold . . .' Like his descendants he may have been fond of horse-racing, but the word 'jockey' was also a form of Jacky, the diminutive of Jack and John, and it was also a convenient name for his enemies to use because 'jockey' in addition stood for a cheat, due to the bad reputation of horse-traders.

John Barleycorn: malt liquor personified (barley from which the drink was made) and extolled in ballads from the seventeenth century. Robert Burns wrote a poem under that title, and in his *Tam o'Shanter*, 1789, he says:

> Inspiring bold John Barleycorn!
> What dangers thou canst make us scorn!

John Bull: personification of the Englishman and his character, beloved (or ridiculed) by writers and cartoonists for his stolidity (in mind as well as appearance), ruggedness and commonsense—sometimes arrogance: usually depicted as an eighteenth-century (when he made his first appearance) or early nineteenth-century country gentleman in riding jacket and top boots, bluff, well-fed. The name was popularised in pamphlets by John Arbuthnot, aimed against France, and published as a book, *The History of John Bull*, 1727. He may have been inspired by the name of the organist and composer John Bull (1563–1628) who is credited with the first composition of the national anthem. Byron mocked:

> The world is a bundle of hay,
> Mankind are the asses who pull;
> Each tugs in a different way,
> And the greatest of all is John Bull.

(Arbuthnot 1667–1735), a Scottish doctor and writer, was a physician to queen Anne whom he dubbed 'Mrs Bull'. He was adept at nicknames: he called the pope 'Lord Peter'.)

John Doe: man-in-the-street q.v., a legal invention from the nineteenth century, using a fictitious name for a plaintiff when preparing or arguing a case, usually in ejectment actions. The hypothetical defendant was referred to as Richard Roe. John Noakes was another name used.

jolly Roger: the pirates' black flag with skull and crossed bones: 'roger' is an obsolete word for rogue (also for a ram).

juggernauts: name applied to the heavy lorries introduced onto the roads, especially the inter-continental goods traffic after Britain joined the 'common market' q.v. The word was used as early as 1912 in an article on motoring in *The Times*. (See Donald Reed, *Edwardian England*, London, Harrap, 1972, p. 119.) Juggernaut is a Hindu idol, taken in procession on a huge carriage once a year.

Jumbo: child's name for an elephant. There was a real Jumbo, an elephant weighing more than six tons in London zoo and sold to Barnum's circus in 1882. It was killed by a railway engine three years later.

K

kaffir king, the: Barnett (Barney) Isaacs Barnato (1852–97), Anglo-Jewish financier and speculator in the Kimberley diamond industry and in South African gold mines. His financial ramifications were known as 'the kaffir circus'. Heavy losses ensued. He jumped from a ship sailing from Cape Town and was drowned.

kevanhuller: laced or braided hat, with brim pinched-in at one side, following a military fashion set by Ludwig Andreas Khevenhüller (1683–1744), Austrian field-marshal whose skill as a commander, especially against the French and Bavarians, was publicised in England (his name variously spelt). 'If the end of a fine lady's dress was not rather ornamental than useful we should think it a little odd that hats, which seem naturally intended to screen their faces from the heat or severity of the weather, should be moulded into a shape that prevents their answering either of these purposes: but we must, indeed, allow it to be highly ornamental, as the present hats worn by the women are more bold and impudent than the broad brimmed staring Kevanhullers worn a few years ago by the men': *The Connoisseur*, No 36, 1754.

king cotton: the profitable and dominating cotton-growing industry in the southern states of America, transferred to the cotton manufacturing of Lancashire when it provided the most employment. (See William Armstrong's novel *King Cotton*, London, Collins, 1947.) See also *cottonopolis*.

king Dick: Richard Cromwell (1626–1712), son of Oliver whom he briefly succeeded as protector, but his incompetence earned him the further nicknames of 'queen Dick' and 'tumbledown Dick' q.v.

Kingledon: the Wimbledon lawn tennis courts, nicknamed thus by the *Daily Mirror* in 1972 in honour of the American player Billie Jean King (née Moffitt) when she won the singles championship for the fourth time. She took the title for the sixth time in 1975 and announced it would be her last appearance. Billie Jean was also one of the greatest doubles players. See *Miss Frigidaire*.

king-maker, the: Richard Neville, earl of Warwick (1428–71), valiant fighter on the Yorkist side against the Lancastrians, secured the throne for his cousin, Edward of York, but because of the king's intrigues Warwick turned against him and for a short period ruled England himself as lieutenant of Henry VI whom he released from prison. Edward defeated his army and Warwick was killed at Barnet. Lord Lytton's novel, *The Last of the Barons*, tells his story.

king of Bath: Beau Nash, q.v.

king of the Cotswolds: Gray Brydges, fifth baron Chandos (c1580–1621), scion of a family tracing its ancestry to a knight who came over with William 'the conqueror', so named because of his lavish hospitality and style of living at Sudeley castle. He was lord-lieutenant of Gloucestershire.

king's evil: scrofula, because it was thought that a touch from the king would cure it, the monarch himself having been annointed and blessed at his coronation. It was practised in England and France, from the reign of Edward III in England, and royalty continued the tradition into the reign of queen Anne. Charles II was estimated to have 'touched' as many as a hundred thousand people, and in Evelyn's *Diary* for 1660 there is a detailed description of the ceremony. The office for the occasion was included in the book of common prayer until 1719. Boswell in his *Life of Johnson* tells how, when the great man was a child, his mother 'yielding to the superstitious notion' took him from Lichfield to London to be 'touched' by queen Anne. Boswell adds: 'This touch, however, was without any effect.' In 1712 the queen placed her royal hands on two hundred people in one day.

king's great matter, the: popular reference at the time to Henry VIII's long drawn-out efforts to get his marriage to Catherine of Aragon annulled so that he could wed Anne Boleyn. See *nun of Kent*.

king's (or queen's) shilling: enlistment in the British army. ('He's taken the shilling.') From the coin given by the recruiting sergeant on a man's agreeing to join up, thus establishing a contract. The standard pay for a private was for long a shilling a day.

kiwis: New Zealanders, the people themselves and their touring sporting teams, from the flightless bird found only in that country and adopted as a national emblem.

knife-board: late nineteenth-century horse-drawn omnibus which had a long centre bench on top, passengers sitting back-to-back, resembling the knife-cleaning board familiar in kitchens.

L

lackland: king John (1167–1216), fourth and youngest son of Henry II and Eleanor of Aquitaine (she was forty-four when he was born) because, unlike his brothers, he was given no feudal possessions in England or France. He was known as John Lackland throughout his youth: his eventful and troublous reign is remembered mainly for Magna Carta. The French nicknamed him 'dollheart' when he fled from the siege of La Roche-aux-Moines in 1214, although he had stronger forces than Louis who was dubbed 'Louis the lion' (in contradistinction with John's brother, Richard 'the lionheart').

lady bountiful: a charitable well-off person, as the squire's mother in Farquhar's comedy *The Beaux' Stratagem*, 1707.

lady of pleasure: see *woman of the town*.

lady with the lamp: Florence Nightingale (1820–1910), philanthropist and nursing pioneer, given this nickname by grateful soldiers whose nursing she organised at Scutari during the Crimean War. By strength of will, skill and administrative ability she reformed the slipshod and insanitary conditions, and inspected the wards at night, carrying her lamp. She made nursing respectable.

lake poets (or school), the: Wordsworth, Coleridge and Southey who lived in, or visited, the Lake District in north-west England and were inspired by its varied beauty, the name used none too kindly by critics at the time. Sometimes called the 'Cumberland poets', although the Lake District spreads over Westmorland and north Lancashire.

lame duck: someone handicapped by misfortune or his own incapacity; a defaulter on the stock exchange by mismanagement or bad luck. It was a stigma to be shunned in nineteenth-century business circles, but became softened in the twentieth. The money-conscious old Mr Osborne in Thackeray's *Vanity Fair* was suspicious of the financial position of Amelia's father: 'I'll have no lame duck's daughter in my family.' (ch. xiii).

land o' cakes: Scotland, famed for its oatmeal cakes. 'Hear, Land o' cakes and brither Scots' sang Robbie Burns.

land of nod: sleep. One does not need to go further for an explanation than the involuntary inclination of the head when 'nodding off to sleep', but some have sought an origin in *Genesis* iv, 'Then Cain went away from the presence of the Lord, and dwelt in the land of Nod, east of Eden', *nod* in translation signifying 'wandering'.

last man, the: Charles I (1600–49), so called by parliamentarians who thought he would be the last of the kings. Royalists rejoindered with 'son of the last man' for Charles II.

last of the English: Hereward 'the wake', q.v.

last of the red hot mommas: Sophie Tucker (1884–1966), American singer and actress, popular in her own country and Britain for her vitality and style of singing in 'variety' and 'musicals'.

last of the Saxons: king Harold (c1026–66) who has perhaps a better claim than Hereward to be 'last of the English', son of earl Godwin; killed at the battle of Hastings when William of Normandy ('the conqueror') invaded to claim the throne.

latitudinarians: those clergy in the Church of England and their sympathisers who were not so much concerned with dogma and orthodoxy as others thought they ought to be—'broad' in their outlook (from the Latin *latus*, broad); applied to the more liberal theologians of the seventeenth and eighteenth centuries. It was the 'latitude' of such people that the later Oxford movement q.v. sought to discipline.

levellers: political group, mainly of soldiers in the parliamentary army during the civil wars, advocating reforms under the leadership of John Lilburne. See *free-born John*.

lion of Judah: Haile Selassie, emperor of Ethiopia (Abyssinia) from 1930 until his dethronement in 1974, with the exception of the Italian occupation, 1936–41. He was a founder of the Organisation of African Unity.

little corporal, the: Napoleon Bonaparte (1769–1821), affectionate nickname by his early compatriots, recalling his humble (but very short) period in an artillery regiment: he quickly became an officer. He was not as 'little' as all that—five feet six inches tall. Describing his appearance in his last years on St Helena, major-general Frank Richardson in *Napoleon's Death: an Inquest*, London, William Kimber, 1974, says: '. . . his corpulence and fat round thighs made him look shorter than he really was. His legs were quite shapely and he was proud of his delicate little hands and small feet.'

little Englander: one who regards England as sufficient in itself, or indicating a narrowness of outlook on the international scene; applied originally to the opponents of imperialism and colonisation in Victorian times. 'Mrs Judith Hart, Minister of Overseas Development and one of the foremost anti-Marketeers in the Government, yesterday answered the charge that the anti-EEC group were merely Little Englanders': *The Guardian*, 8 May, 1975.

little Mo: Maureen Connolly, American tennis player and a favourite at Wimbledon where she won the championship three times, 1952–4. She won her first championship at Forest Hills in 1951, when only sixteen. Her tennis career ended after an accident in 1954.

little sure-shot: Annie Oakley (1860–1926), a remarkably accurate markswoman from childhood in America. She joined

Buffalo Bill's 'wild west' show and toured with it in the USA and Europe. On a visit to England in 1887 queen Victoria saw her performance. One of her tricks was to shoot a hole in a playing card thrown into the air, so that the nickname for a punched ticket was an 'Annie Oakley'. The musical play *Annie Get Your Gun* was based on her story.

little Willie: (1) Friedrich Wilhelm, crown prince of Germany, eldest son of the kaiser of the First World War, so named by British troops. He commanded an army group, followed his father into exile in Holland, renounced his right of succession, 1918, (2) a little boy's penis, Will being a nickname for the male organ from the sixteenth century and used as such by Shakespeare in his sonnets. (See Eric Partridge, *Shakespeare's Bawdy*, London, Routledge & Kegan Paul, 1968.)

lollards: fourteenth-century nickname for followers of John Wycliffe (see Wycliffites), but used earlier in Holland for a group of Franciscans who questioned the authority of the pope, hence a possible explanation for the word—from old Dutch meaning to hum or to sing softly (cf. our own 'lull' or 'lullaby') or from a word meaning an idler (cf. 'loll'). It is interesting to remember that in the seventeenth century the Independents often expressed appreciation of a sermon by humming. But a strong contender in the derivation puzzle is *lolium*, tare, a poisonous weed. Chaucer must have had this source in mind when the shipman in *The Canterbury Tales* speaks of 'This Loller heer wil prechen us somwhat...Or springen cokkel in our clene corn.' Lollards aroused much enmity during Wycliffe's lifetime and after. Gower in his *Confessio Amantis*, 1393, referred to

> This newe secte of lollardie
> And also many an heresie

And John Audley early in the fifteenth century wrote: 'Lef thou me, a Loller, his deeds they will him deem ... Never for him pray.' (Take it from me, a Lollard is known by his deeds ...)

lollipop lady (or man): warden of a pedestrian crossing with special responsibilities for children, carrying a pole with a red warning disc on top which could be likened to the lollipop sweet of juvenile delight.

longshanks: Edward I (1239–1307), eldest son of Henry III, a tall, handsome warrior-king who also did his best to re-organise the administration of his country as well as keep Wales and Scotland in order. See *hammer of the Scots.*

long Tom: two guns and a president: a forty-two pounder gun captured by the English from a French ship in 1798 and sold to America; a naval gun used by British troops against the Boers in the South African war (1899–1902); and Thomas Jefferson (1743–1826), third president of the USA, whose career was followed by British newspapers, a tall lawyer-turned-politician who helped to draw up the declaration of independence, 1776.

Lord Fanny: unkind nickname given by Pope to John Hervey, baron Hervey of Ickworth (1696–1743), vice-chamberlain to George II and lord privy seal, statesman and clever writer who made several powerful enemies, including Horace Walpole as well as Pope. He criticised the court, was involved in intrigue and fought a duel. Mentally adroit, he was physically weak, suffered from epilepsy and maintained a rigid diet which his opponents ridiculed. He was said to have used cosmetics, hence Pope's nickname: others he gave him were Sporus, Adonis and Narcissus. Pope is said to have been jealous of his friendship with lady Mary Wortley Montagu.

Lord Haw-haw: William Joyce who broadcast Nazi propaganda from Hamburg during the Second World War, speaking in a cultured voice which the *Daily Express* radio correspondent ridiculed with this nickname, and it was widely adopted, a valuable antidote to the subversive messages of German victories and intentions that Joyce put over. He was hanged for treason in 1946. Cf. Tokyo Rose q.v.

Lord Porn: Francis Aungier Pakenham, seventh earl of Longford, politician and reformer, one time leader of the house of lords under a Labour government and lord privy seal, notorious for his vigorous campaign against pornography and sexual licence. In 1972 he headed an unofficial group inquiring into pornography and the decline of moral standards. He urged higher penalties for pornographic offences, a new definition of the law of obscenity, a clean-up of books, films and television programmes, and the banning of sex education in schools without parental consent. A great publicist for his causes (which included rehabilitation of prisoners) he was sometimes dubbed 'the holy fool'.

(Pornography goes far into history, long before eighteenth-century Casanova q.v., the marquis de Sade and Nicolas Edme Restif—called Restif de la Bretonne—French novelist whose *Le Pornographe*, 1769, proffered a plan for regulating prostitution and whose massive memoirs of amatory exploits shocked a generation; but Lord Longford's concern was that sexual exploitation was widespread and open.) See *permissive society, sexy sixties*.

Lothario: a philanderer, seducer or rake, from the character of that name in Nicholas Rowe's *The Fair Penitent*, 1703. See *Casanova, Don Giovanni, Don Juan*.

lotus-eaters: those who live in luxury, standing aside from life and usually living abroad, hedonists in dreamful ease; an extension from the ancient Greek belief in a Libyan tribe that ate a fruit which produced a happy forgetfulness, a pleasurable idleness. Homer tells of Odysseus reaching such a country where many of his sailors ate the lotus and lost all desire to return home.

love days: because of their intended amicability, the days appointed in medieval times for the clergy to settle disputes by arbitration. In his prologue to *The Canterbury Tales* Chaucer writes of the friar:

> And rage he couthe right as it were a whelpe,
> In love-dayés ther couthe he mochil helpe.

Which suggests that such arbitrations were not always friendly affairs.

Lovell the dog: Francis, viscount Lovell (1454–87), lord chamberlain to Richard III and a loyal supporter, so that he was derided as the king's spaniel. His enemies circulated a rhymed couplet around London:

> The catte, the ratte and Lovell our dogge,
> Rulyth all England under a hogge.

The 'rat' was Sir Richard Ratcliffe, the 'cat' Sir William Catesby, speaker of the house of commons, and the 'hog' was the king himself because he had a white boar on his coat-of-arms.

lowbrow: one who is not erudite, whose tastes are simple and unintellectual: accepted with 'highbrow' q.v. as a respectable word, as in a caption to a cartoon in *The Sunday Times*, 18 May, 1975, commenting on Scottish culture and nationalism, 'I'll take the highbrow and you'll take the lowbrow', parodying the well-known song, 'I'll take the high road . . .'

lower deck: inferiors, from the naval reference to those below commissioned rank, quartered on the lower decks.

lucifer: a friction match invented by John Walker (c1781–1859), a druggist of Stockton-on-Tees; persisting as a name for all matches to the end of the First World War during which a popular song included the verse:

> Pack up your troubles in your old kit-bag,
> and smile, smile, smile.
> While you've a lucifer to light your fag,
> smile boys, that's the style . . .

See *congreves, vestas.*

luddites: unemployed workers and those fearing loss of jobs because of the introduction of machinery, rioting and wrecking factories in the midlands, the disturbances spreading to northern counties, 1811–16. Mechanisation was causing great distress. A nickname for the secret ringleaders was captain Ludd, or king Ludd, the name—so the story goes—originating accidentally from that of a Leicestershire boy called Ned Ludd who was caught up in the troubles. See also *captain Swing.*

M

macaronis: late eighteenth-century dandies, men-about-town, addicted to gambling, drinking and duelling. A Macaroni Club was started in London about 1760 by young men who had made the tour to Italy (see 'grand tour') and professed a liking for that country's speciality of wheaten flour moulded into tubes. The word persisted into the next century as a nickname for elegant fops.

Mac the knife: Harold Macmillan when as prime minister in 1962 he sacked seven cabinet ministers. See also *supermac*.

mad poet, the: Nathaniel Lee (c1653–92), dramatist as well as poet. He wrote plays in verse and a tragedy, *The Rival Queens*, which had some success. Hard drinking affected his brain and he was confined to Bedlam for a time.

mae west: inflatable life-jacket issued to the services in the Second World War, the nickname coined by the RAF in tribute to the curvaceous American film star, Mae West (b. 1893) and then adopted as the official description, with the full approval of the buxom lady. Mae West, gay and uninhibited, first came into prominence in the film *She Done Him Wrong*, 1933, based on her play, *Diamond Lil*. Her catch phrase, 'Come up and see me some time' was for long on people's lips.

(It is interesting to recall that an earlier American actress with a plump figure, Lillian Russell (1861–1922) gave her name to a fashion popular in England as well as in her own country. The 'Lillian Russell' ensemble beautified the hourglass figure, with sweeping bosom and a gown with a train,the lady wearing a large Gainsborough hat bedecked with feathers or flowers.)

mafficking: uproarious celebration, as in the case in Britain when news came through that Mafeking, besieged by the Boers, had been relieved in May, 1900. The defence by Baden-Powell for seven months had aroused the public imagination and anxiety, and the relief brought out the wildest enthusiasm in the streets, adding a new word to the language. The news was received on the night of 15 May: it was announced from theatre stages, shouted from omnibuses: there was dancing in the streets, bands playing, flags at windows: railway engines blew their steam whistles all over the country, ships hooted their horns in the ports. Excitement was intense, and there were processions next day.

magpie houses: half-timbered houses of the Tudor period, the framework of black-painted wood and white plaster likened to the magpie's colouring, designs ranging from utilitarian simple to elaborate ornate. Some of the best remaining examples are in Cheshire and Shropshire.

mahogany: what Boswell in his *Life of Johnson* describes as 'a curious liquor', favoured by Cornish fishermen, composed of two parts gin and one part treacle, well-beaten together. 'I thought it very good liquor, and said it was a counterpart of what is called Athol porridge in the Highlands of Scotland, which is a mixture of whisky and honey.' (Given here only because of the unusual constituents and the little-known name: the many nicknames for drinks—black velvet, for example, a mixture of stout and champagne—are omitted from this dictionary.)

maid of Orleans: Joan of Arc (1412–31), French heroine of history and legend, who was inspired to lead the troops in the relief of Orleans, besieged by an English and Burgundian army. She was eventually captured and burned in the market place at Rouen. Her canonisation as St Joan did not come about until 1920. The French call her *La Pucelle*.

maltworm: a drunkard, of very old origin, at least as early as the sixteenth century; from the weevil that infests malt, hence a consumer of malt liquor. In I *King Henry IV*, (II, i), Gadshill speaks of 'these mad mustachio purple-hued malt-worms'.

Manchester school, the: advocates of free trade and repeal of the corn laws, a movement of which Richard Cobden, John Bright and Charles Villiers were leaders, their campaigns based in Manchester where great meetings were held. Disraeli probably invented the name in 1848. The city's Free Trade Hall, also famous as the home of the Hallé orchestra as well as a forum, commemorates the movement which in addition became identified with a pacific foreign policy.

man in leather breeches: George Fox (1624–91), founder of Quakerism (see *Quakers*), a nickname bestowed on him in his early years as an itinerant preacher. He walked or rode throughout Britain and his reputation was such that people called 'The man in leather breeches is come!' The reference to his attire, always neat and clean, is not clear: leather breeches were not uncommon. He may have made them himself: as a boy he was apprenticed to a shoemaker and he worked with leather. He records the nickname in his *Journal*.

man-in-the-street: the elusive ordinary citizen whom politicians court and in theory revere. Many attempts have been made to elicit his views on current affairs, the most striking innovation being Mass-Observation, a form of widespread personal inquiry invented in the nineteen-thirties by Charles Madge and Tom Harrisson, recording opinions and answers to questions. Opinion polls, letters to newspapers, *vox pop* interviews for radio and television, and 'phone-ins' for broadcast programmes have extended the investigation. *The Observer*, 13 July, 1975, recalled an old court case in which an attempt was made to describe a representative citizen: 'Abiding by the nineteenth century judicial definition of the reasonable man—"the man on the Clapham omnibus"—we boarded a Clapham-bound bus in search of judgments on the Government's £6-a-week proposals.' (In reference to efforts to control wage increases.)

man of letters: a writer, a literary scholar.

man-of-the-world: a sophisticated person, one who has 'been around'. The name was popularised by a comedy of that name by Charles Macklin (1781), Irish actor and playwright. See *panjandrum*.

marsh, the: medieval nickname for the rush-strewn floor of the great hall, below the level of the dais on which the lord and his family sat. This part of the hall would often be muddy as retainers tramped in, also from food discarded, drink spilt and perhaps the ordure of dogs.

maypole, the: Ehrengard Melusina von der Schulenburg, duchess of Kendal (1667–1743), German mistress of George I, disrespectful nickname given by the British public because she was tall and thin. She followed George to England and he bestowed on her several British and Irish titles.

media, the: a misinvention beloved of politicians in the nineteen-seventies, used *ad nauseam* in reference to the mediums of communication—newspapers, radio and television—usually critically.

merry Andrew: a jester, clown, from the assistant to a 'quack' q.v. doctor who fooled around on fairgrounds to attract attention. A theory of derivation is that it commemorates Andrew Boorde (or Borde), an eccentric physician, formerly a monk, who died in 1549. He travelled extensively, wrote about his journeys and the countries he visited, as well as about diet. He was said to have practised at country fairs. Several jest-books are credited to him, perhaps wrongly. He was imprisoned for keeping prostitutes in his house.

merry monarch, the: Charles II (1630–85), because of his own light-hearted character (although seriously inclined towards the arts and invention, and tolerant in religion) and the relaxation of the restoration years in contrast with the puritan restrictions of Cromwell's time. John Wilmot, second earl of Rochester, who was adept at writing amorous poems and rude verse, satirised Charles and his mistresses and described him as 'A merry monarch, scandalous and poor'. As a child, Charles was nicknamed 'the black boy' because of his dark colouring, a fact that surprised his mother, Henrietta Maria.

merry Monday: the day before shrove Tuesday. See also *St Monday*.

merrythought: the furcula, the v-shaped bone on a bird's breast, commonly known as 'the wishbone' because of the old custom of taking the bone from a roasted or boiled fowl, two people grasping it with the little finger, the one breaking-off the larger part being granted his secret wish.

Merry Widow hat: a large hat festooned with feathers, as worn by Lily Elsie in the musical play, 'The Merry Widow'. It fascinated the ladies, but annoyed men sitting behind one in a theatre or encountering such on a crowded pavement. 'Merry Widow Hat Danger. Worse Than Sweep's Brush, says Solicitor': headlines in the *Evening Chronicle*, Manchester, 1907.

Methodists: nickname given in 1729 to members of the 'holy club' q.v. at Oxford University and which was honourably adopted, becoming an identification (as with 'Quakers' q.v.) for a religious movement, the word arising from the strict regularity of bible study and worship by John and Charles

Wesley, George Whitefield and other undergraduates—the methodical way in which they observed their principles. Wesleyan Methodism began with John in 1744, although both he and Charles remained in the Church of England, the movement not becoming a separate denomination until 1795.

middle ages, the: like the 'dark ages' q.v. a convenient expression for a period of imprecise length, variously interpreted in European history as between the fifth and fifteenth centuries, from the collapse of the Roman empire to the 'renaissance' q.v., or until the reformation in the early sixteenth century—a thousand years or so.

miss: this contraction of 'mistress' has been tossed about between the scandalous and the respectable, used for a lady of easy virtue as well as for a very proper unmarried woman. In his *Diary* for 9 January, 1662, John Evelyn refers to an actress's last appearance on the stage, 'she being taken to be the Earl of Oxford's *Miss* (as at this time they began to call lewd women)'. By the end of the century it was an accepted euphemism. A broadsheet of that time amusingly defines the word: 'A miss is a new name which the civility of this age bestows on one that our unmannerly ancestors called whore and strumpet. A certain help mate for a gentleman instead of a wife; serving either for prevention of the sin of marrying, or else as a little side pillow to render the yoke of matrimony more easy.' (Quoted from Philip Pinkus, *Grub Street Stripped Bare*, London, Constable, 1968.)

Victorians and Edwardians revived, but softened, the connotation of the word, always with an emphasis—'She's a *miss!*', meaning the person was either naughty or daring, or perhaps just unconventional; and it was often used for a self-willed little girl. (My grandmother, who died in 1927, and her contemporaries gossiping over cups of tea, were still using the word in this way. V.N.)

Miss Frigidaire: Chris Evert, American tennis player, winner of the women's singles championship at Wimbledon, 1974, noted for her deliberate and unruffled—and usually unsmiling—style. Reporting on her losing to Billie Jean King in the semi-final of 1975, David Gray in *The Guardian*, 3 July, wrote: 'As we watched her (Mrs King) wearing down Miss

Evert, destroying the superfine accuracy of the cold girl from Florida, we were conscious again that Mrs King is the most remarkable of post-war champions ...' There followed remarks by Mrs King about her love for Wimbledon, and Gray went on: 'How could Miss Evert, the fair Miss Frigidaire, prim and accurate, hope to counter a player who cared as much as that?' Mrs King won the championship for the sixth time. See *Kingledon*. (Mrs King paid tribute elsewhere to Miss Evert's warmth off-court and her sense of humour.)

missing link, the: in zoology the much sought-for intermediate form of animal between anthropoid apes and man; rudely used as a nickname—mainly among heartless schoolboys —for someone who may have an unfortunate appearance or has offended in some way. In a review of a biography of the eminent zoologist, Louis Leakey, *The Guardian*, 15 May, 1975: 'Two or three million years had been added to the estimated age of the human species and Africa accepted as its birthplace; several new hominids ('missing links' as they were once called) identified ...' Various names have been given to ape-men whose fossilised bones have been found, such as the famous 'nutcracker man'.

mistres of the seas: Great Britain in the days of her naval supremacy, especially in the nineteenth and early twentieth centuries.

moaning Minnie: the air raid warning siren of the Second World War, summoning citizens to take shelter; also soldier's nickname for a German mortar shell, *minnenwerfer*.

mob, the: contraction of *mobile vulgus* (fickle crowd) and invented as a nickname by members of the Green Ribbon Club (see *'green ribbon men'*) around 1680 who incited public anti-Catholic demonstrations with 'pope-burning' bonfires.

mods and rockers: two groups of young people, often in opposition; teenage cults arising in the nineteen-sixties. The mods were fashion-conscious, tending to ride scooters when out and about; the rockers, girls as well as boys, sported more 'masculine' gear, jeans and leather jackets, and rode motorcycles. There were some violent clashes when the groups met at roadside cafés and seaside resorts, police making arrests. See *rockers*.

mohocks: eighteenth-century gangs of well-to-do ruffians, especially in London, named after the Mohawk Indians, rampaging in the streets, assaulting pedestrians, sometimes overturning coaches. Steele in *The Spectator*, No. 324, 1711, gives horrifying details of the behaviour of what he calls 'the Mohock club' and says: 'An outrageous ambition of doing all possible hurt to their fellow-creatures is the great cement of their assembly, and the only qualification required in their members. In order to exert this principle in its full strength and perfection, they take care to drink themselves to a pitch that is beyond the possibility of attending to any motions of reason or humanity . . . Some are knocked down, others stabbed, others cut and carbonadoed. To put the watch to a total rout, and mortify some of those inoffensive militia, is reckoned a *coup-d'éclat*'. He goes on to list atrocities—squashing of noses, gouging of eyes, piercing of legs with swords, indecent assaults on women. These gangsters were also called hawkubites.

Moll cut-purse: Mary Frith, a seventeenth-century notoriety who often dressed as a man on her robbing expeditions, and even held up general Fairfax on Hounslow Heath: a highwaylady. She made a small fortune out of crime and was able to buy herself out of Newgate. She died of drink, aged seventy-five. She is commemorated in Samuel Butler's *Hudibras* (first part published in 1663, the last 1678), with a change of vowel for the sake of rhyme:

> A bold virago, stout and tall,
> As Joan of France, or English Mall.

Molly Maguires: members of an Irish secret society around 1843, men who put on women's clothes to surprise and terrorise rent collectors. They fought against evictions.

molotov cocktail: improvised anti-tank bomb made from a bottle filled with petrol and topped by a slow fuse, beloved of the Home Guard (see *'Dad's army'*) in the early part of the Second World War. When thrown, the burning liquid could spread over a tank, with possible delaying results. Named after the Russian revolutionary and former underground fighter, V. M. Molotov who became chairman of the council of the people's commissars, 1930, commissar for foreign affairs, 1939–46, then foreign minister.

monks of Medmenham Abbey, the: nickname given to a group of dissipated young gentry in the eighteenth century who called themselves Franciscans, after their leader, Sir Francis Dashwood. They were otherwise known as 'the hell-fire club'. They met at Dashwood's home on the Thames, near Henley. Boswell called them 'a riotous and profane club'. Lord Sandwich (see '*Jemmy Twitcher*') and John Wilkes were among the members, sharing Dashwood's violent and wanton youth. Dashwood (1708–81) became chancellor of the exchequer and fifteenth baron Le Despencer.

Mons Meg: a fifteenth-century cannon at Edinburgh castle, made at Mons.

moonlighters: an Irish secret society towards the end of the nineteenth century; also a nickname for people who quit their homes at night, removing furniture, to evade rents and debts; hence the term, 'moonlight flit'.

moon's men: thieves and highwaymen operating at night. Shakespeare in I *King Henry IV* (I, ii) has Falstaff and prince Henry playing with the words, the former saying, 'for we that take purses go by the moon', and the latter, 'for the fortune of us that are the moon's men doth ebb and flow like the sea . . . a purse of gold most resolutely snatched on Monday night and most dissolutely spent on Tuesday morning . . . now in as low an ebb as the foot of the ladder, and by and by in as high a flow as the ridge of the gallows.'

Moravians: a protestant community tracing its history to John Huss (1373–1415), given the convenient name because of its country of origin. After many vicissitudes, some members came to England in the seventeenth century, finding a congenial climate for worship and gradually establishing settlements as bases for itinerant preachers and missionary efforts, first in London and the south, then in the north, notably Manchester and Pudsey in Yorkshire. Keen educationists, they started schools, a famous one the Fulneck Schools (boys and girls, boarders and day pupils), Pudsey, established 1753.

Mormons: members of the Church of Jesus Christ of Latter-Day Saints, the name given because the founder, Joseph Smith, published *The Book of Mormon*, 1830, claiming to be divinely inspired from a golden volume he dug up on a hill in

New York State. When Smith and his brother were shot by a mob, Brigham Young became leader and guided his people across the prairies from Illinois to Utah and established Salt Lake City as its capital, 1847. Missionary zeal has always been characteristic of the church, and such work began in England as early as 1837.

morocco men: touts and sub-agents for eighteenth- and early nineteenth-century state lotteries who went about the country with impressive books bound in red leather in which speculators' names were entered: a receipt was given which did not always count for much. There was a flourishing business for contractors who bought tickets in bulk, at a discount, and sold them in shares. You could buy a ticket for £15 (with a chance of winning £20,000) or a share in a ticket for as little as three shillings, 'to afford' as one advertisement put it, 'a fair and legal opportunity for persons in every station in life to adventure upon a secure, advantageous and permanent foundation'.

morrison: an indoor air raid shelter recommended by the government in the Second World War, named after Herbert Stanley Morrison when he was home secretary and minister of home security, 1940–45. He became baron Morrison of Lambeth. See *anderson*.

mortar-board: the square-topped cap worn with an academic gown, likened to an upturned mortar (a vessel in which substances are pounded) on a board. The French have a similar word, *mortier*, which was a cap worn by ancient kings, and that of the president of a court of justice. The English etymology is not clear, the nickname perhaps coming from the board on which a builder carries mortar. See also *trencher cap*.

mosquito armada: the fleet of little ships—from rowing boats to pleasure steamers—which set out from British ports to join the royal navy in evacuating survivors of the British expeditionary force from the beaches around Dunkirk in 1940. Between the end of May and 4 June 338,000 allied troops (two-thirds British) had been ferried across the channel under attack so that they could fight again—a defeat turned into a victory. The ships were later honoured by being able to fly the cross of St George.

moss troopers: bandits, marauders who infested the boggy borders ('moss' meaning peat bog or spongy land) between England and Scotland from the mid-seventeenth century.

mother of parliaments: the house of lords and house of commons, or the British parliamentary system as copied in the commonwealth and empire: an extension of a remark by John Bright in 1865 that 'England is the mother of parliaments.'

mother of the maids: the senior of the maids of honour at court, the chaperon, probably an older married woman; from Elizabeth I. In his *Diary* for 2 June, 1662, Evelyn refers to such an office in connection with Charles II's queen, Catherine of Braganza: 'Now saw I her Portuguese ladies, and the Guardadamas, or Mother of her Maids.' He did not think much of their attractions, because earlier he had commented on 'a train of Portuguese ladies in their monstrous fardingales . . . their complexions olivander and sufficiently unagreeable'.

Mrs Grundy: a symbol of social convention, a censorious person, upholder of morals, from Thomas Morton's sentimental comedy, *Speed the Plough*, in which one of the characters frequently asks what would Mrs Grundy say.

mud-larks: nineteenth-century nickname for scavengers at low tide on the Thames in London, usually children or old destitute people. Henry Mayhew in his philanthropic surveys, *London Labour and London Poor* (1851–64) referred to their plight. In *London: the Biography of a City*, London, Longman, 1969, Christopher Hibbert comments: 'They went down into the mud by the banks of the Thames carrying old hats or rusty kettles, poking about for pieces of coal or copper nails, their clothes a collection of old rags stiff as boards, their feet bare and in danger of being cut on fragments of buried glass.' See also *street arabs*.

Muggletonians: one of the many dissenting sects of the seventeenth century, led by Lodowicke Muggleton (1600–98) who claimed that he and his cousin, John Reeve, had a divine mission. He was imprisoned and fined for blasphemy.

mug-house: nickname for a tavern or ale-house, from the days when it was customary in many places to pass round a mug of beer (usually a wooden container) to which drinkers contributed. In such group drinking there were quarrels, and in the reign of king Edgar (944–75) among the many laws passed was one ordering pegs to be placed in mugs at even spaces to ensure that each person got a fair share; which suggests that the saying, 'Take him down a peg' is a thousand years old. Does the slang word 'mugging' for assault go as far back?

muscadins: early nineteenth-century Parisian fops whom English visitors to the city were startled to see aped what they considered to be English manners—loud voices, swaggering, vulgarity of speech. Byron referred to them in *Don Juan* viii: 'Cockneys of London! Muscadins of Paris!' See also *goddams*.

N

naked fashion, the: nickname for a style of dress at the end of the eighteenth century and beginning of the nineteenth when muslin was in vogue, and transparent (or nearly so) gowns were worn, both outdoor and indoor, with little or no underclothes. Dresses were of Grecian simplicity, low-cut, high-waisted, often with the skirt slit to the waist at one side revealing a leg in pink stocking. Some daring females even damped the muslin before taking a walk so that it clung closely to the figure. 'There is so little to be concealed at present that there is scarcely room for any fashion at all' said the *Chester Chronicle* in 1801; and on another occasion, 'The only sign of modesty in the present dress of the Ladies is the pink dye in their stockings, which makes their legs appear to blush for the total absence of petticoats.' (Quotations taken from Mass-Observation *Browns and Chester*, London, Lindsay Drummond, 1947).

Like most other things, it was not new. In a letter to *The World*, No 21, 1753, complaint was made about 'nakedness in fashion' among young ladies: 'It is the fashion for a lady to *undress* herself to go abroad, and to *dress* only when she stays at home and sees no company.'

namby-pamby: Ambrose Philips (c1675–1749), both praised and ridiculed as a poet, the nickname bestowed on him by Henry Carey, making play with his name. Carey, Pope and

Swift thought his pastorals and his verse generally had received attention far beyond their merits; but Addison and Dr Johnson had a higher regard for his work. He edited a whig magazine in London and was an MP and a judge in Ireland. This is another example of a nickname becoming a dictionary word, meaning a delicate, protected, insipidly sentimental person.

nation of shopkeepers: England, according to some people, and Napoleon—who used the phrase derisively (*boutiquiers* was his word)—was certainly not the first. He borrowed it from his fellow Corsican, the freedom-fighter Pasquale Paoli (1725–1807) who may in turn have read it in Adam Smith's *The Wealth of Nations*, 1776.

NATO: North Atlantic Treaty Organisation, formed by the USA and eleven European countries for collective security, 1949; joined in 1952 by Greece and Turkey.

naughty nineties, the: by hindsight, the eighteen-nineties when there was an outburst of unconventional behaviour among the younger middle class, a relaxation of Victorian prejudices, more audacious writing for the stage, and the popularity of the music-hall; and there was the *Yellow Book* (1894–7) to which Oscar Wilde contributed among other 'modern' authors, and, Aubrey Beardsley and Max Beerbohm provided drawings.

navvy: this contraction of 'navigator' for a man employed on digging canals became a general name for a labourer using pick and shovel. In the era of canal construction in the eighteenth and early nineteenth centuries these waterways were called 'navigations', and their designers—like James Brindley—were the 'navigators', the word extending to the labourers they employed, and later to those who dug the foundations and tunnels for the railways.

nazis: members of the national socialist German workers' party, shortening of *Nationalsozialistische Deutsche Arbeiterpartei*, developed from 1920 under the leadership of Adolf Hitler and Ernst Roehm. It became the 'hate' word in Britain, and in his many speeches during the Second World War, Winston Churchill pronounced it with a particular venom.

NEDDY: National Economic Development council, 1962.

Nell of old Drury (or sweet Nell): Nell (or Eleanor) Gwynn (1650–87) who sold oranges around the Theatre Royal, Drury lane, London, and became an actress and mistress of Charles II by whom she had two sons. She appears to have been a gay, generous and warm-hearted person, illiterate but intelligent. Pepys called her 'pretty, witty Nell' and Dryden wrote parts for her. Evelyn wrote of her disapprovingly as 'Mrs Nelly, as they called an impudent comedian.' Charles's death-bed request, 'Let not poor Nelly starve' was faithfully kept by his brother, James II, who settled her debts and provided money and an estate.

nessy: the mysterious creature (or creatures) believed by many people and from long local legend (going back to the sixth century) to inhabit loch Ness in Scotland; promoted for the sake of tourism but also the subject of much scientific investigation, including underwater exploration. Photographs of a seemingly aquatic animal with a snake-like head and two humps have been taken. Public interest was first aroused by the report of a sighting from a motorist along the shore in 1933, but serious attention was not devoted to 'nessy' until the post-war years, especially in the nineteen-sixties and 'seventies. Theories have ranged from that of prehistoric monsters trapped in the loch to otters, optical illusions and sheer fantasy.

nest-egg: savings or investments for future requirements, such as retirement, perhaps from the custom of placing a pot egg in a hen's nest to encourage her to lay.

new look: a fashion introduced by the Paris couturier, Christian Dior, in 1947 which delighted women accustomed to the austere dresses of wartime. As a reaction to the severe lines of uniform and the frowning on frivolity, the 'new look' brought back the old attractions of feminine curves, recognisable waists and long full skirts.

new morality, the: a term fashionable in the nineteen-sixties to indicate the abandonment of 'middle class morality' in favour of freedom from conventional restraints. There was questioning of religious concepts and a declining influence by the Christian church, marked by a lack of self-discipline in sexual and other matters; altogether a rather negative attitude. See *permissive society* and *sexy sixties*.

new woman, the: she emerged towards the end of the nine-teenth century and the beginning of the twentieth and was given this name because of the novelty of seeing her abandon-ing convention, bicycling with men, attending dances without a chaperon, seeking higher education, taking an office job (the first typists were called 'lady typewriters'), asserting her individuality, and—above all—campaigning for the vote. She was even seen to smoke a cigarette! She usually came from various strata of the middle class, her poorer sister being accustomed to work already, if not to taking part in public affairs. See *shrieking sisterhood, suffragettes*.

new world, the: the American continent after the voyages of discovery beginning in the fifteenth century.

nickleodeon: this American nickname for the early cinema (admission a nickel, five cents) was not adopted in Britain until the nineteen-thirties when a coin-in-the-slot music machine was introduced, followed by a popular song making play with the word.

noble science, the: better described as 'the noble art of self-defence', referring to fencing and boxing, but more generally applied to the latter.

Noll: diminutive of Oliver and the nickname given to Oliver Goldsmith (1728–74) by his friends, among whom was David Garrick who is credited with this epitaph:

Here lies Nolly Goldsmith, for shortness called Noll,
Who wrote like an angel, but talked like poor Poll.

Dr Johnson admired him greatly, as did Horace Walpole who nevertheless described him as 'an inspired idiot'. Boswell records: 'It has been generally circulated and believed that he was a mere fool in conversation; but, in truth, this has been greatly exaggerated. He had, no doubt, a more than common share of that hurry of ideas which we often find in his country-men, and which sometimes produces a laughable confusion in expressing them.' Boswell, in his *Life of Johnson*, was referring to Goldsmith being an Irishman.

116

no-man's-land: the territory between opposing forces, the term used by British and allied troops during the trench warfare, 1914–18.

nonconformists: general name for protestant bodies which do not conform to the church of England; members of the dissenting movement against the established church which began in the reign of Elizabeth I. When the act of uniformity was passed in 1662, enforcing strict observance of the book of common prayer, about two thousand clergymen were ejected from their churches.

nonconformist conscience: a nineteenth-century jibe at those who adhered to a 'puritan' outlook on society, especially frowning on drinking and gambling and upholding a 'middle class morality'. In *Lady Windermere's Fan*, 1891, Oscar Wilde joked, 'There is nothing in the whole world so unbecoming to a woman as a nonconformist conscience.' It was largely such a conscience in the house of commons that persuaded Mr Gladstone to suggest to Parnell, after he had been accused of adultery, that he should resign his leadership of the Irish party for the sake of home rule and politics generally. (See *'uncrowned king of Ireland'*.) The 'conscience' was strong and well represented in the Liberal government of 1906; and it was behind many social reforms.

nosey: (1) Oliver Cromwell (1599–1658) whose nose was bulbous and often red, which earned him the additional nicknames of 'copper nose' and 'ruby nose'; (2) soldiers' nickname for the first duke of Wellington (1769–1852) because of his prominent, aquiline nose—sometimes 'old nosey'.

nun of Kent (or holy maid of Kent): Elizabeth Barton (c1506–34), a neurotic girl who claimed to have visions both before and after her admittance to a convent at Canterbury, attracting considerable attention. She embroiled herself in politics and prophesied that Henry VIII would die 'a villain's death' if he divorced Catherine and married Anne Boleyn. (Who put her up to it?) She continued her treasonable utterances after the marriage, was examined before star chamber and 'confessed'—by pressure and torture, perhaps—and with others was executed at Tyburn. See *the king's great matter*.

117

Nuremberg eggs: egg-shaped silver watches made in this Bavarian town from the sixteenth century. They were among the many items of Nuremberg craftsmanship in metal, wood and ivory—including decorated guns, astrolabes and globes—which spread its fame throughout Europe.

O

oak boys, the: gangs of youths in Ulster around the mid-eighteenth century who protested against tithes and other taxes. They wore oak leaves in their hats.

Offa's dyke: a long earthwork from the mouth of the river Dee, near Prestatyn, to the Wye near Monmouth, constructed by the order of Offa, king of Mercia, who died in 796, as a boundary between his domain and the Welsh.

Old Bill: a cartoon character created by Bruce Bairnsfather in the First World War, a whiskered, cheerful soldier who became the embodiment of the grumbling but irrepressible infantry-man. Most famous was the drawing of Bill and a comrade taking refuge in a shell-hole, Bill saying: 'Well, if you knows of a better 'ole, go to it.' One of the first 'talkies' q.v. (before Al Jolson's sensational debut) was a Warner Brothers 'short' called *The Better 'Ole* with Syd Chaplin as Old Bill and synchronised war songs. 'Better 'ole' became a catch phrase, and Old Bill persisted for a time as a nickname for an old soldier.

old country, the: affectionate name for Britain given by her citizens in the far-flung countries of the world, and by their descendants born abroad.

old Dutch: a beloved wife, short for 'duchess', probably of Cockney origin. The comedian Albert Chevalier (1861–1923) spread the nickname with his song, *My Old Dutch*—'There ain't a lady living in the land as I'd swap for my dear old Dutch.'

old glad-eye: William Ewart Gladstone (1809–1898), statesman and prime minister (see *grand old man*) as he was known by the *demi-monde* of London for his crusading efforts in the reformation of prostitutes, some of whom he took home to try to turn them from their way of life. It was noted that he usually selected the pretty ones. He was familiar with some of the higher echelon of Victorian courtesans, including the notorious Skittles (Catherine Walters) whose salons he attended, along with the prince of Wales, Lord Kitchener and aristocracy. See Henry Blyth *Skittles: the last Victorian Courtesan*, London, Rupert Hart-Davis, 1970.

old glory: the American flag, the 'stars-and-stripes' q.v., popularised in Britain through fiction and films.

old Grog: see *grog*.

old groaner, the: see *groaner*.

old guard, the: (1) pioneer loyal supporters of a party, people who stubbornly adhere to principles, though possibly outworn; (2) veteran regiment of Napoleon's imperial guard, elite of the army, devoted to him and considered invincible, so that when they fell back at Waterloo demoralisation set in among the other troops. Just as Napoleon himself had his admirers among Englishmen, so had his guardsmen and their exploits.

old lady of Threadneedle street: the bank of England, because of its London location since the eighteenth century. See *Throgmorton street*.

old masters: usually denoting pictures painted by famous artists which have retained their high regard among critics— and their prices; also the artists themselves.

old nick: one of the many nicknames for the devil, this one older than most. It has a long history, going back to *nicker*, the water goblin with hoofs in Scandinavian legend. (A poetic Norse name for a lake was *nykraborg*.) The word is used in the oldest of English narrative poems, the Beowulf saga. In a translation by Henry Morley a couplet reads:

> Naked high nesses,
> Nicker houses many.

There have been various spellings during the English transformation of a condemned water spirit (with an ear for music) into the master of hell—nichus, necker, nek among them. In Grimm's *Teutonic Mythology* the name is translated 'neck', and Matthew Arnold's poem about the lonely creature from the sea who sought human comfort and a chance to regain heaven is entitled *The Neckan*. All are related.

old pretender, the: James Francis Edward Stuart (1688–1766) son of James II and acknowledged by his followers and Louis XIV of France as James III, but not by the English people. His attempts to gain support in the country failed and he spent his life in exile, dying in Rome. See *warming pans, young pretender*.

old Rowley: Charles II (1630–85), the nickname having two explanations—one being that it came from the name of his favourite stallion in the royal stud at Newmarket (with reference, perhaps, to the king's own sexual prowess), the other that it was based on the ancient legend of the two stalwart knights, Roland and Oliver, who exchanged blow for blow, hence the phrase 'a Roland for an Oliver'. The latter meaning would seem appropriate, England having found a Roland (Rowley) in exchange for an Oliver (Cromwell), but it seems far-fetched.

old school tie: privilege arising from the friendship in leisure, politics, business and the professions of those educated at the same public school or university, identified by their wearing the same kind of tie. It has been used both in the sense of class loyalty and as a term of envy or derision.

old world, the: the eastern hemisphere in distinction from America, the 'new world' q.v.

one-armed bandit: the gambling 'fruit' machine (its symbols on the revolving wheels being coloured fruits) and similar automatic contraptions operating by the insertion of a coin and the pulling of a lever: a 'bandit' because the chance of winning much is very low.

one-leg Paget: Henry William Paget, first marquess of Anglesey (1768–1854) who, as Lord Uxbridge, a cavalry officer, lost his right leg at Waterloo. The story goes that in the battle he suddenly exclaimed, 'By God, sir, I've lost my leg!' to which Wellington replied, 'By God, sir, so you have!' and continued his direction of hostilities. The partly severed leg was amputated, placed in a coffin and buried in a garden in the village of Waterloo.

OPEC: Organization of Petroleum Exporting Countries, an acronym which immediately became a word, used in the house of commons as such.

open house: everybody welcome.

opium eater, the: Thomas de Quincey (1785–1859), author and essayist, who led an unsettled though productive life and who acquired a taste for opium while at Oxford—taken to allay neuralgia. His *Confessions of an English Opium Eater*, 1822, introduced him to a wide public—a book of considerable literary merit as well as being self-revelatory.

orangemen: members of the Orange Order, founded in Ulster in 1795 with the aim of maintaining the protestant constitution. The name commemorates William of Orange, who became William III and who defeated the army of exiled James II at the battle of the Boyne, 1690.

orange Peel: Sir Robert Peel (1788–1850) who was secretary for Ireland at the age of twenty-four, and although trying to hold a balance was compelled to show protestant bias, and later in the house of commons led the opposition to Roman catholic emancipation. His attitude changed, however, and in 1829 he backed the emancipation cause in a speech of more than four hours.

orator Hunt: Henry Hunt (1773–1835), radical politician, prominent at public meetings wearing the white hat of the reformer. He tried unsuccessfully to become a member of parliament, but was not elected (for Preston) until 1830. In the meantime he had been imprisoned for conspiracy, arrested at the historic open-air meeting in Manchester which became known as the 'Peterloo massacre' q.v. Later he championed women's rights and presented the first petition of this kind to Parliament. See *women's lib*.

Oriana: one of the several names for queen Elizabeth I, used in masques and madrigals.

oscar: nickname for the statuette awarded each year by the American Academy of Motion Picture Arts and Sciences for distinction in acting, writing and production. There are several explanations for the word, none being generally accepted.

outer space: the region beyond the gravitational pull of the earth, a term popularised with the beginning of planetary exploration in the nineteen-sixties.

Oxbridge: a convenient composite of Oxford and Cambridge to denote the characteristics of the two older universities, their traditions, the kind of men they produce; sometimes used in distinction from 'redbrick universities' q.v. Thackeray may have invented the word, but it did not come into general use until the post-Second World War years.

Oxford bags: extremely wide-bottomed trousers, an oddity of men's fashion introduced at Oxford university in the nineteen-twenties and for a short time adopted by other young men. The trousers flared to skirt-like absurdity and soon lost their attraction.

Oxford group, the: name given to a small number of men, mainly from Oxford university and trained by Dr Frank Buchman to lead a spiritual re-awakening against materialism, when they visited South Africa in 1928. The name invented by the South African press persisted until the movement became known as Moral Re-armament (MRA) ten years later. See *Buchmanites*.

Oxford movement, the: a high church movement originating at Oxford university, 1833–41, under the guidance of E. B. Pusey, John Keble, R. H. Froude and J. H. Newman, arguing for the teaching and practice of the early and undivided church, a truly 'catholic' church of England, but not Roman catholic. There was a call for return of some of the ceremonial and ritual that had fallen into disuse. See *Puseyites* and *tractarians*.

P

panjandrum, the great: a mighty personage, or one who considers himself such, derived from a word invented by Samuel Foote (1720–77), actor and dramatist. The distinguished Shakespearean actor, Charles Macklin—noted especially for his portrayal of Shylock—boasted that he could memorise anything after one reading. Foote challenged him by composing a nonsense passage with inconsequential happenings (presaging Lewis Carroll) in which 'the great panjandrum' appeared. Foote's friends thought it a good joke, but Macklin was not amused, considering the effort too ridiculous to bother about.

pantaloons: nickname for tight trousers (in the regency period, fastened below the shoes) as worn by Pantaloon in the early pantomimes, the knock-about butt of the clown's fun. He had a long ancestry, going back to Italian comedy in which he was often a crusty old gentleman, with Columbine as his daughter, Harlequin his servant.

paper tiger: one who is not as fierce as he looks, like the paper animals in carnival processions; sometimes applied to a threat, or even a country. (Paper is a convenient word—like 'paper' money, for banknotes; 'paper' profits, for figures shown on financial statements, hypothetical profits.)

parsley Peel: Robert Peel (1750–1830), wealthy Lancashire cotton manufacturer who inherited his father's calico-printing firm and became father of the more famous Sir Robert Peel. This elder Robert was also a member of parliament. One of his best-selling fabrics had a parsley pattern which became very fasionable, prompting his workpeople to invent the nickname which spread to those 'in the know' in the rest of the country.

parson's nose: the rump of a fowl, the nickname giving parishioners a chance to make fun of their vicar; also *pope's nose.*

pathfinders: specially-trained bomber crews, their aircraft equipped with the latest navigational devices, who flew ahead of the main bombing force in the latter part of the Second World War to identify and light-up the target; formed in 1942 under the command of air commodore D. C. T. Bennett, formerly a station commander in 4 group of bomber command, the pioneer night bombing group.

paul pry: an inquisitive, meddlesome, interfering kind of person, from the comedy *Paul Pry* by John Poole (1785–1872).

Paul's man: a show-off with little justification, a boaster, a gossip-monger. The centre aisle of St Paul's, London, before its destruction in the fire of 1666, was the haunt of idlers and a promenade for the pseudo-fashionable in search of the gossip of the town, as well as for the down-at-heel. Business was also transacted in 'Paul's walk', as it was known, and for a time servants could be hired there. A scene in Ben Jonson's comedy, *Every Man Out of his Humour*, 1599, is set in Paul's walk. See *bobadil*.

pearlies, costermongers in the east end of London who, from about 1875, began to decorate their clothes with pearl buttons on festive occasions, a custom that grew into a tradition, with elaborate designs on suits and dresses and the election of 'pearly kings' and 'queens'. They carried out much charitable work. In acknowledgment of their part in London life their representatives were officially received in the house of lords, May, 1975.

peculiar people: a small Christian sect, forerunners of Christian Scientists in their belief that bodily ills could be cured without professional medical help, founded in London by John Banyard in 1838. They relied on prayer and good nursing, and came under criticism when members—or their children—died without a doctor's attention.

peeler: a policeman, named after (Sir) Robert Peel when he was secretary for Ireland early in his career and founded the Irish constabulary. Later, as home secretary in England, he instituted the metropolitan police force and the nickname was adopted for its members. See *bobby, charlies, redbreasts*.

peeping Tom: usually applied to one whose sexual interest prompts spying on female privacy, a voyeur; from the story of Lady Godiva's naked ride, through Coventry in 1040—a challenge from her husband Leofric when she pleaded for relief of taxes for the citizens. After her ride on horseback with only her long hair as covering the earl kept his promise. The occurrence developed into a more detailed legend, describing how the grateful populace stayed indoors behind closed shutters in deference to her modesty—all except one, a tailor called Tom who took a peep and was struck blind.

peep o' day boys: one of the many Irish secret societies, this one protestant and noted for its dawn raids on Roman catholic communities in the latter part of the eighteenth century. As always, violence begot violence, and the catholics formed a society of 'defenders' to counter these incursions.

penguins: an RAF nickname for officers with 'flying' rank (pilot officer, flying officer, flight lieutenant, squadron leader, etc.) who did not usually fly but had ground duties; also—on some airfields, but not generally—members of the WAAF (Women's Auxiliary Air Force).

penny-a-liner: a free-lance journalist contributing news stories to papers, his payment calculated according to the number of lines used; for many years the rate was a penny.

penny dreadfuls: cheap papers ('comics') for boys, and similar magazines with lurid stories, from Victorian times on. G. K. Chesterton wrote an essay defending them, maintaining that criticism against them was exaggerated. 'These common and current publications have nothing essentially evil about them,' he wrote. 'They express the sanguine and heroic truisms on which civilisation is built.' The name persisted for this type of publication long after the price for blood-and-thunder increased, but with the coming of decimalisation it fell out of use.

penny-farthing: the 'new' bicycle of 1872 because of the large front wheel and a small back one, resembling the two coins. It became the 'ordinary' as opposed to the 'safety' bicycle with its wheels of equal size.

Perdita: see *fair Perdita*.

permissive society: a term applied in the nineteen-sixties to a change in moral attitudes (some argued that it was a laxity of moral standards), with a more liberal outlook on sexual relationships, including homosexuality; the proliferation of gambling and strip-tease clubs; outspoken comment on intimate relationships between men and women in books and plays in the theatre and on television. It was also the period of the mini-skirt and the introduction of the contraceptive 'pill' q.v. See also *sexy sixties*.

Peterloo massacre: the occasion in August, 1819, when an open-air meeting on St Peter's field, Manchester, was dispersed by cavalry with drawn swords, eleven people being killed and scores severely injured. With the battle of Waterloo only four years previously the name seemed appropriate. Banners proclaimed 'Annual Parliaments', 'Universal Suffrage', 'No Corn Laws'. There had been a royal proclamation against 'seditious' meetings, and local magistrates had warned against this one. When 'orator Hunt' q.v. began to speak from a cart, the mounted yeomanry—many of them drunk, it was said—were sent in, scattering men, women and children alike.

Peter's pence—a levy of a penny per family with a certain minimum income paid to the pope annually, instituted in the eighth century, but the exact date is not certain, originally for the upkeep of an English school in Rome. The tax was paid fairly regularly, with a few lapses, until Henry VIII abolished it in 1534.

petro-dollars: an invention of 1974 for the currency demanded by the oil exporting countries (OPEC q.v.) which had greatly increased their prices, with disastrous economic results in Britain and elsewhere.

Piccadilly weepers: see *dundrearies*.

pickpocket, pickpurse: a thief. 'Pick-purses in love and we deserve to die': *Love's Labour's Lost* (IV, iii). See *Moll cut-purse*.

picts: painted ladies, a nickname coined by Steele in *The Spectator* No 41, 1711, from the ancient Scottish tribes who indulged in war paint. In a tirade against make-up he wrote: 'The muscles of a real face sometimes swell with soft passion, sudden surprise, and are flushed with agreeable confusions . . .

But the Picts behold all things with the same air, whether they are joyful or sad; the same fixed insensibility appears upon all occasions. A Pict, though she takes all that pains to invite the approach of lovers, is obliged to keep them at a certain distance; a sigh in a languishing lover, if fetched too near her, would dissolve a feature; and a kiss snatched by a forward one, might transfer the complexion of the mistress to the admirer.'

Picts' wall: another name for Hadrian's wall q.v.

pilgrimage of grace: a rising led by Robert Aske in 1536 in protest against the dissolution of monastries and political moves by Henry VIII. Aske occupied York and captured Pontefract castle, and with thousands of his fellow Yorkshire-men and others from Lincolnshire planned to march on London, but was persuaded by the king's promises to halt at Doncaster—promises which were not kept. Implicated in another rebellion led by Sir Francis Bigod he was hanged for treason in the following year.

pilgrim fathers: the founders of Plymouth colony, Massachusetts, in 1620, most of them puritans from Lincolnshire, some of whom fled to Holland for freedom of worship. They set sail from Plymouth in the Mayflower, seventy-eight men and twenty-four women. The name was first given to them about a hundred years later.

pilgrims' way: the road from Winchester to Canterbury which pilgrims to the shrine of Thomas Becket took after his canonisation in 1173, not long after his murder in the cathedral. It was at Winchester that pilgrims gathered for the journey, not only from the south and west of England but from across the channel by way of Southampton. The road follows a very ancient track.

pill, the: oral contraceptive, introduced in the nineteen-sixties, unique of its kind and marked out from every other pill by the definite article: in its own way, a social revolution. 'Call to sell the pill over the counter': headline in *The Times*, 15 May, 1975.

pin money: a wife's allowance for personal expenditure, or her own small earnings. The term is of very old origin, recalling the days when pins for utilitarian and decorative purposes were expensive: it largely fell out of use after the Second World War when it became customary for many married women to take jobs and earn their own pin money.

placemen: members of parliament, civil servants, court officials and the like who held offices of profit, often as a result of patronage; men who held 'places' with monetary rewards in return for the support they could give.

plague Sunday: the annual commemoration in August at the Derbyshire village of Eyam of the disaster which occurred in 1665–66 and the fortitude and self-discipline of its inhabitants. Plague broke broke out—due, it is thought, to infection from a consignment of cloth from London—and quickly spread through the close community. Inspired by their gallant rector (whose wife died) the villagers agreed to remain in isolation so as not to spread the disease. Out of a population of 350, 260 people died.

plantagenet: the nickname given to Geoffrey, count of Anjou (1113–51) became the surname of a dynasty. It was said that he had a habit of wearing a sprig of broom (*planta genista*, or *genet*) in his cap, or that he planted broom. He also had the honorific of *le bel*, the handsome. His eldest son by his wife Matilda became Henry II of England, 'the first of the Plantagenets'.

platform: a policy for which a political party—or protagonist of a cause—stands, as on a platform.

plon-plon: prince Napoleon Joseph Charles Paul Bonaparte (1822–91), second son of Jerome Bonaparte (a brother of Napoleon) who commanded a division in the Crimean War, soldiers' translation of *plomb-plomb*, or *craint-plomb* (fear lead). It was an unkind nickname given him after the battle of Alma when his courage under fire was questioned, probably without justification.

plot night: 5 November, commemorating the plot to blow up the houses of parliament in 1605 and the arrest of Guy Fawkes; one of the oldest of public 'celebrations' consistently observed, with fireworks and the burning of a 'guy'.

Plymouth brethren: religious sect of which John Nelson Darby was a founder, the evangelical work beginning in

Plymouth and Dublin around 1830. Small groups were formed for bible study and worship, meeting in houses and halls. See *Darbyites*.

pocket battleships: the warships, small but powerful, that Germany built after the First World War, supposedly keeping within the limits of ten thousand tons as stipulated by the treaty of Versailles.

pocket borough: a parliamentary constituency under the control of a local man, landowner or squire—having the voters 'in his pocket', whether by payment or persuasion.

pocket dictator, the: Engelbert Dollfuss, who became chancellor of Austria in 1932 and tried to unite all parties against the Nazi threat. He was assassinated two years later. The nickname used in the British press came from his very small stature.

pom (or pommy): Australian nickname for an Englishman (and often for other residents of Britain) and used to a lesser extent in New Zealand. Partridge *DSUE* accepts it as slang and suggests it is a simple corruption of Tommy. (See *Tommy Atkins*.) There have been many attempts to explain the derivation, some fanciful. Australians employed it in fairly friendly fashion until the assisted-passage scheme for immigrants after the Second World War and the upsurge of Australian nationalism, when in many cases it was uttered with a sneer. (In an Australia-bound ship in 1973 I heard it used only derogatively, sometimes extended to 'Ten pound poms'. V.N.)

pons asinorum: the asses' bridge, fifth proposition of Euclid, book one, familar to—and unloved by—generations of schoolboys who found it difficult to cross.

pooh bah: an officious dignitary or one holding many offices, as did the gentleman of that name in Gilbert and Sullivan's *The Mikado*.

posh: acronym of 'port out, starboard home', these letters entered on the booking forms of P & O liners against the names of first-class passengers making the return voyage to

India who could afford to pay extra for cabins on the cooler side of the ship to escape the heat of the Indian ocean. The word became synonymous with privilege in the days of the British empire, and was transferred into colloquial speech to indicate someone of higher standing than the rest, even with pretence to grandeur. (I am aware that Eric Partridge *DSUE* proposes different explanations, but I prefer this one.)

postman poet, the: Edward Capern (1819–94), long-forgotten but meriting a mention in *DNB*. He was a Devonshire postman who had previously worked in a lace factory. His verses were first published in 1856 and attracted favourable attention because of their imaginative simplicity on rural themes.

potteries, the: the Staffordshire area in and around Stoke-upon-Trent, famous for the manufacture of earthenware of all kinds, and including Hanley, Tunstall, Burslem, Fenton, Longton and Etruria, and with which the families of Wedgwood and Minton are outstandingly identified. It was at Etruria—named after the ancient district of Italy, noted for its inhabitants' skills in metalwork and pottery—that Joseph Wedgwood founded his business in 1769 and built a village for his workpeople.

pre-Raphaelites: the 'brotherhood' of artists formed in 1848 by William Holman Hunt, J. E. Millais and D. G. Rossetti and joined by F. G. Stephens, T. Woolner, W. H. Deverell and J. Collinson to establish a simpler and more 'naturalistic' style of painting than was in vogue at the time, their pictures—for the most part—characterised by high colours and minute detail. They at first agreed to sign their pictures **PRB**. They shocked most of the critics, except Ruskin who gave encouragement.

press, the: newspapers in general, from the printing press (the pressure of inked type on paper), a transfer of meaning first used in the late eighteenth century. Before that the extension had been mainly to publishing houses and the issue of printed books, pamphlets, etc. When Goldsmith used the term 'the press' in *Letters to a Citizen of the World*, 1762, he was referring only to book publication.

Pride's purge: the occasion in 1648 when colonel Thomas Pride arrested forty-five members of the 'long' parliament and prevented many others from entering the house of commons because they were in favour of reconciliation with Charles I. The remainder were called 'the rump'. Pride's was one of the signatures on the king's death warrant.

prince of macaronies: George Bussy, fourth earl of Jersey (1735–1805) who held several offices at the court of George III and was noted for his elegant manners and fastidious tastes. See *macaronies*.

prince of wails: Johnny Ray, one of the first American 'pop' singers in the post-Second World War years to arouse British teenage audiences to hysterical fervour—a frenzy of screams—the nickname given both for this achievement and to his vocal style.

prinny: George IV when prince of Wales. See *first gentleman of Europe, Florizel, Fum the fourth*.

prisoner of Spandau, the: British press nickname for Rudolf Hess (b. 1894) who became Hitler's deputy. He surprised the world in May, 1941, by flying to Scotland, ostensibly to try to arrange a separate peace between Germany and Britain. By the end of the war his mind seemed to be unbalanced, and he sat through the war crimes trial at Nuremburg as if not understanding what was going on. He was condemned in 1946 to life imprisonment, and in the nineteen-seventies efforts were made to obtain his release from Spandau prison on humanitarian grounds.

private eye: a private detective, Americanism quickly adopted in Britain, popularised in films and television programmes. Typical: '. . . private-eye Mike Hammer is hired by secret service men to investigate the murder of another agent': *Radio Times*, 20 July, 1975.

props: the diminutive of 'properties', used to describe the articles necessary in the production of a play.

Puffing Billy: nickname which became the title for one of the earliest steam locomotives relying on friction between wheels and rails for movement (instead of the rack rail), built by

William Hedley in 1813, slightly pre-dating George Stephenson's more efficient and sophisticated Rocket.

puritans: originally a satirical nickname for the extreme sixteenth-century protestant clergy who wished to 'purify' the Church of England of what they regarded as superstitious and corrupt practices retained from Roman catholicism. They argued against ceremonies and traditions in matters of worship which were not according to the scriptures. The name was adopted for the whole body of people of Calvinistic outlook and theology and a strict way of life.

puritan Sunday: a sabbath of strict religious observance and austerity, especially as practised during the seventeenth-century commonwealth when all sport and entertainment was forbidden. Ordinances proscribed various activities offensive to the Lord's day, including 'vainly and profanely walking'. These lapsed at the restoration and during Charles II's reign 'puritan' was often a dirty word. Sunday observance acts got into their stride from 1625: that of 1781 prohibited any public entertainment for which admission was charged, the places being classed as 'disorderly houses'. Not until 1932 was it made lawful for local authorities to sanction Sunday cinemas and musical entertainments. The Lord's Day Observance Society has for long been active, often clashing with public opinion. The continental term was 'the English Sunday'.

purple heart: (1) a pill of that shape and colour favoured by drug-takers, c1950 on; (2) American term, familiar in Britain, for the heart-shaped medal suspended from a purple ribbon (with white edges) awarded to US servicemen wounded on duty.

purple patches: highly-coloured prose in works of fiction or other writing; the overabundance of adjectives and florid description, often amatory; perhaps recalling the ancient significance of purple as a symbol of luxury and power.

Puseyites: followers of Edward Bouverie Pusey (1800–82), one of the leaders of the Oxford movement q.v. and centre of theological controversy for his 'high church' views. Although he was not entirely in sympathy with it, the revival of pre-reformation ceremonial of worship was a characteristic of the movement.

pussyfoot: an advocate of temperance or complete abstinence from alcohol, the word derived from W. E. 'Pussyfoot' Johnson (1862–1945), an American who worked tirelessly in the cause of prohibition. He got his nickname from his stealthy methods in prosecuting law-breakers in the gambling saloons.

Q

quack: an itinerant drug seller at fairs who 'quacked' forth the praise of his wares, a shortening of 'quacksalver' which produced the nickname and from which we get 'quack doctor', a pretender to knowledge of medicine, or at least an unconventional one. The word probably came from the German *quaken* or the Dutch *kwakken*, to croak (like a duck). A report from the country to *The Connoisseur*, No. 23, 1754, gives a picture of a quack and his assistant: 'About the middle of last month there came among us one of those gentlemen who are famous for the cure of every distemper, and especially those pronounced incurable by the faculty . . . when I considered his impassioned speeches, and the extempore stage from which he uttered them, I was apt to compare him to Thespis and his cart. Again, when I beheld the Doctor dealing out his drugs and at the same time saw his Merry-Andrew play over his, tricks, it put me in mind of a tragi-comedy.' See *merry Andrew, toad-eater.*

Quaker poet: (1) Bernard Barton (1784–1849), a bank clerk who attained some distinction with his verses, friend of Lamb and Southey; (2) John Greenleaf Whittier (1807–92), American poet whose work is perhaps best-known in Britain in hymnals.

Quakers: a nickname of derision given to the early followers of George Fox (1624–91) which they accepted and which the movement retained after it adopted its own title of the Religious Society of Friends and has been synonymous ever since; cf. Methodists q.v. When Fox was charged with blasphemy at Derby in 1650 he told the magistrate, 'Tremble and quake at the name of the Lord!' The magistrate replied: 'You quake, do you? Quakers, eh?' In the biography of Fox, Vernon Noble, *The Man in Leather Breeches*, London, Elek, 1953: 'The term that Bennett (the magistrate) scoffingly used quickly became popular, as if people had hitherto not regarded Fox's followers as a separate sect but were now eager to give them an identification.' See also Fox's *Journal*. Strangely, the name was not new: it had previously been used for highly emotional puritans; but it was adopted as new for a people who suffered severe persecution meekly, who lived their religion, without dogma or ceremony, who practised silent worship and believed in a direct awareness of God—the 'inner light'—without the intermediary of a minister. They were at one time the largest of the dissenting sects, but although their numbers dwindled their influence in social reforms over the centuries far outweighed their membership.

queen Dick: Richard Cromwell (1626–1712), son of Oliver, an alternative nickname to 'king Dick', this one given because of his timidity and inability to cope with events during his brief rule following his father's death; but there was also a hint of homosexuality, probably unfounded. He left for Paris in 1660 and sought a quiet life under the name of John Clarke, returning to England twenty years later where he died in comparative obscurity. See *tumbledown Dick*.

queen Sarah: Sarah Churchill (née Jennings), duchess of Marlborough (1660–1744), because of her influence at court: she had been a favourite attendant of queen Anne since the latter was a princess. She played an important part both in her husband's rise to wealth and power and in his fall from grace. While on the closest terms with the queen they called each other in private conversation Mrs Freeman and Mrs Morley. Sarah's cousin, Abigail Hill, succeeded her in the queen's favour.

queen's day: during the reign of Elizabeth I the date of her accession to the throne in 1558—17 November—was observed as a public holiday under this name.

queer Hardie: (James) Keir Hardie (1856–1915), a founder and chairman of the Independent Labour party, a Labour member of parliament and a man of great integrity and character; a play on his name and in recognition of his quirks, such as wearing a cloth cap. *Punch*, 3 July, 1912, called him 'Don't Keir Hardie'. Bernard Shaw described him as 'the damndest natural aristocrat in the house of commons'.

quickie: a film produced cheaply and with more rapidity than prestige films with big names, so as to bring in a quick return for outlay.

quisling: a traitor, fifth columnist q.v., the word adopted into the language from Vidkun Quisling, former minister of defence in Norway who formed a national union party and who supported the invasion of his country by the Germans in 1940. He became minister-president under the Nazi occupation, head of a puppet government. After the German defeat he was tried and shot in 1945. The noun will no doubt become as firmly established as the verb 'to boycott', after C. C. Boycott (1832–97), the Irish land agent who was ostracised.

R

Rab's boys: name given to a team working under R. A. Butler to reform the Conservative party after its defeat in the post-war election of 1945 and moulding it into a strong opposition. The team prepared a programme for industry, with the aim of full employment, co-operation between workers and employers, wages related to productivity, greater security for workers; free enterprise but accepting some nationalisation schemes. Controls were criticised and lower taxation urged. In the Conservative victory of 1951 Butler became chancellor of the exchequer.

rachmanism: exploitation of house tenants, with extortion, a word used in courts and at rent tribunals following a London scandal of this kind in the nineteen-sixties in which a Peter Rachman was the centre.

radar: coined from 'radar detection and ranging'—first known as radiolocation—experiments beginning in 1935 by the direction of air ministry and developed under Robert (later Sir) Watson Watt; a technique of using radio waves to 'bounce back' a signal onto a cathode-ray screen. By the outbreak of the Second World War a chain of radar stations was in operation to detect approaching aircraft, their position and distance, an early warning of inestimable value for ground defence and for directing fighter 'planes. As the chain was rapidly extended it replaced the sea, in the age of air war, as a defence of our shores—the sea which for long had served 'in the office of a wall, or as a moat defensive to a house', as Gaunt put it in *King Richard II*. Radar was installed in aircraft and ships for detection and navigation to targets. See *bogeys*.

raglan: a loose coat, sleeves extending to the neck, no seams on the shoulders, as worn by Lord Raglan (1788–1855), a soldier who lost a hand at Waterloo and who commanded the British forces in the Crimea where he died of dysentery.

railway king, the: George Hudson (1800–71), son of a farmer who became a draper in York and mayor of the city, a member of parliament and founder of a banking company. He was involved in the development of railways, made a fortune, but lost that and his reputation by over-speculation and questionable activities.

rainbow corner: nickname given by American servicemen to Lyons Corner House, Shaftesbury avenue, London, when it was converted into a club for them during the Second World War, probably because of the variety of insignia of its visitors.

raree-show: name given to a peep show in a box carried around the streets, and at fairs from the seventeenth century. Savoyards who came to England were travelling showmen and they specialised in this type of amusement. *ODEE* suggests the word may have come from their pronunciation of 'rare show'. The German *raritätenkasten* meant a box of rareties. John Evelyn in a letter of 1696 wrote of the house to which he had retired (at Wotton) as 'the raree-show of the whole neighbourhood'.

rat-race: the struggle to keep going in a competitive society, to survive as do rats who fight their fellows for food or who win a race while the losers are destroyed: extended to indicate the conditions of high-pressure living.

red baron, the: Manfred Freiherr von Richthofen (1892–1918), German fighter pilot of the First World War, not only a hero to his own side but greatly respected by the allied airmen. He flew a red Fokker 'plane and led what became known as 'Richthofen's circus' which created havoc. When he was shot down over allied lines he was given a military funeral, with a bearer party of six captains and a firing party provided by the Australian Flying Corps.

redbreasts: nickname given to the Bow street runners, special officers attached to Bow street police court in London who were both writ-servers and detectives. They were disbanded when the metropolitan police force was founded in 1829. They wore a blue coat with brass buttons, usually open and displaying a red waistcoat. They were also called 'robin redbreasts'. See *bobby, charlies, peeler.*

redbrick: applied to universities other than Oxford and Cambridge (see *Oxbridge*), especially those which proliferated after the Second World War, although the term had been introduced by professor Edgar Allison Peers in 1943. It became an accepted term, although glass, steel and concrete were more predominant than brick which had first replaced the stone of the older institutions. Commenting on criticism of a commercial television 'quiz' programme *The Daily Telegraph*, 29 November, 1975: 'A Granada spokesman denied bias to Oxford and Cambridge in the programme, and said many teams from "Redbrick" universities had taken part.'

redcaps: nickname for British military police, with red covers on their caps.

redcoats: until the general introduction of khaki, the nickname for British soldiers of the line because of their scarlet tunics. 'The publican 'e up an' sez, "We serve no red-coats here" ': Kipling, *Barrack Room Ballads*, 1892. The wearing of red goes back to the early part of the civil wars when Cromwell introduced the colour for his troops. Antonia Fraser, *Cromwell Our Chief of Men*, London, Weidenfeld and Nicolson, 1973: 'It was symbolic of the new feeling for uniformity and discipline that all the Parliamentarian soldiers were now to be dressed in red. "Redcoats all" a newspaper called the New Model Army in May, with only the facings, such as the blue of his family colours for Fairfax's own, to distinguish the various regiments.' Cavalry, however, wore buff leather coats during battle. In the American war of independence, George Washington's troops irreverently called the British 'lobsters'. See *thin red line*.

red dean, the: Dr Hewlett Johnson (1874–1965), former dean of Manchester who became dean of Canterbury in 1931 and was often the centre of controversy because of his political views and his genuine belief that the communist ideal was akin to Christian world brotherhood. He travelled widely, including tours of Russia and China, his last visit to China when he was ninety.

red letter, the: (often called 'the red letter scare'). See *Zinoviev letter*.

reds: communists, a term in general use since the end of the First World War when applied to the Bolsheviks, although the colour red has been associated with social revolutionary movements for much longer, red signifying blood and the spilling of it to gain political ends. It has led to such phrases as 'reds under bed', indicating the suspicions and fears of opposing factions, and 'the red scare'. *The Observer* 31 August, 1975: 'Anyone who thinks that in taking pains to document the influence within the Labour Party of the Trotskyist Revolutionary Socialist League *The Observer* is suffering an attack of Reds-under-the-bed hallucination ought to understand the present anxiety within the Labour Party.'

It is a convenient word, as in *The Guardian*, 21 February, 1975: 'For the truth is . . . that the Industry Bill is neither a red nor a radical measure, save in one possible regard . . .' The international socialist song, 'The Red Flag', words by Jim Connell, was adopted as a 'signature tune' by the British Labour party—'The people's flag is deepest red, it floated o'er our martyred dead, and e'er their limbs grew stiff and cold, their life's blood dyed its every fold.' But red has not been the only revolutionary colour in England. During the early commonwealth it was green, and dissenting soldiers—including the levellers q.v.—wore green emblems.

(Red is also a colour of warning, on 'danger' signs and on the debit side of account books—'in the red'.)

redshirts: the volunteer army recruited by the Italian patriot, Guiseppe Garibaldi, also known as 'Garibaldi's thousand'. His long and adventurous career as a freedom fighter, and the sympathy that Britain had for Italian liberation movements, made him well-known through newspapers. During an interval in fighting, in 1864, he visited London, was given an enthusiastic reception and the freedom of the city.

reformation, the: like 'renaissance' q.v. a small-package convenient word to describe a vast movement which revolutionised religious and political thought in the sixteenth century, out of which grew protestantism and the reconstruction of western Christendom. The smouldering discontent against the doctrines, rites and practices of the medieval church was set alight by Luther's repudiation of the sale of indulgences in 1517. In England, as elsewhere, papal authority was questioned.

regulars: members of the armed forces who have adopted service life as a career, or 'signed on' for a stated period, in contrast with volunteers for 'the duration' of a war, or with conscripts.

remonstrants: presbyterian Scots who presented a 'remonstrance' in 1650, refusing to acknowledge Charles II until he had stated his agreement to the convenants establishing their form of worship. They had cause to be suspicious of a king who commented that presbyterianism was 'no religion for a gentleman'. See *covenanters*.

renaissance, the: a convenient way of shortly describing a mighty and widespread revival of learning (a re-birth, as the word indicates) and its influence on art and literature in the fifteenth and sixteenth centuries; the re-vitalising of European thought and attitudes at the close of the so-called 'middle ages' q.v., humanism and scientific invention breaking away from strict religious dogma, a freer exercise of men's minds and a broadening of outlook through exploration, experiment and discussion.

restoration, the: re-establishing of monarchy with the return of Charles II in 1660, so significant an event that it was applied to the whole of his reign and various activities were identified with it, especially the 'restoration comedies', with their particular frivolity and wit.

resurrection men: robbers of graves and tombs in order to sell the recently interred bodies to surgical and medical schools for dissection in the latter part of the eighteenth century and the beginning of the next. 'Body snatching', as it was called, was briefly profitable and led to even worse crimes, the most notable being that of William Burke and William Hare who killed people and sold the bodies to an Edinburgh surgeon. Hare turned king's evidence, and Burke was hanged in 1829.

Reynard: a fox, the name going back to folklore and twelfth- or thirteenth-century French, Dutch and German literature, the fox and his animal companions—with stories at first founded on Aesop fables—lending themselves to satire on human behaviour in church and state. The cycle of Reynard stories, with Bruin the bear, Tibert the cat, etc., has a fascinating ancestry. The fox was called Renart in the medieval *Roman de Renart,* and Caxton's *The Historye of Reynart the Foxe,* 1481, was a translation from the Dutch.

ribbon societies: groups of catholics in Ireland, wearing a green ribbon as a badge, formed in Ulster around 1820 and spreading south, as defence against the depredations of 'orangemen' q.v. They were active for fifty years or so.

roaring boys, the: gangs of Tudor ruffians, precursors of the 'mohocks' q.v. in a later century and many other lawless youths.

roaring forties: seamen's name in the days of sail for the stormy parts between the fortieth and fiftieth latitudes, north and south, but especially that region in the north Atlantic.

roaring twenties: by hindsight, the nineteen-twenties, surface gaiety returning after wartime gloom, girls 'letting their hair down' (and closely cropping it), raising their skirts from ankle length in 1919 to just below the knee by 1925, vigorously dancing, defying restraints, worshipping Rudolph Valentino on the films, laughing at Mickey Mouse. It was the time of cocktail parties for the better-off; of shoes instead of clogs for mill girls who could afford the flesh-coloured rayon stockings; of put-and-take and other crazes; and at the end of the decade the coming of the 'talkies' q.v. (But there was another side to the picture, slump following boom, and the general strike of 1926.) Cf. *bright young things* q.v.

robin redbreasts: see *redbreasts*.

rockers: groups of young people from the late nineteen-fifties who established a style and a cult, fans of rock 'n' roll 'pop' music, vigorous in their dancing, wearing 'unisex' q.v. clothing. Boisterousness often led to violence, especially when meeting 'mods' q.v.

Romeo: a young man admired by girls and conscious of it, a young lover, as Romeo with Juliet in Shakespeare's play. The epithet has been extended to mean a philandering 'lady killer'. Shakespeare's story was preceded in 1562 by Arthur Broke's poem about the lovers, *The Tragicall Historye of Romeus and Iuliet*, translated from the French version of an Italian original.

Roscius: a talented actor, as was Quintus Roscius Gallus (c126–62BC) whose graceful manners and diction became proverbial. He excelled in comic parts. Cicero was one of his great admirers. Several actors have been compared with him, including David Garrick (1717–79) who was given the honorific, 'the English Roscius'. There was also 'the young Roscius', William Henry West Betty (1791–1874), who first appeared on the stage (in Belfast) at the age of twelve, had great success in Dublin and in Scotland, and appeared at Covent Garden, London, in 1804 when the crowds that gathered to see him were so large that troops had to be called out. On one occasion Pitt adjourned a sitting of the house of commons so that members could see him at the theatre. He had a few years' fame as a boy actor, retired in 1808, returned to the stage four years later, but the glamour was wearing off. He amassed a large fortune.

roundheads: nickname given by the cavaliers to parliamentarians and their troops in the Civil Wars because of their close-cropped hair in contrast with the royalists' longer locks. The term of derision was extended to cover all Cromwell's troops and the civil authorities behind them, even though many of the latter wore their hair to their shoulders. Cromwell himself wore his hair fairly long.

Rowley: see *old Rowley.*

royal martyr, the: Charles I (1600–49), beheaded at Whitehall on 30 January, a date which for long was commemorated. He met his death with great dignity.

rubber stamp: an impersonal acknowledgment or communication; the dealing with a routine matter that requires only a stamp of certification or approval, or a name embossed on a rubber stamp instead of a personal signature by pen.

Rufus, William: William II (c1056–1100), king of England, third son of William 'the conqueror', his nickname-surname arising from the high, swarthy colour of his skin, part of the unattractiveness of his appearance. Contemporaries described him as bull-necked, fat and awkward in his walk, suffering from a stutter which made him difficult to understand when he was in a temper. (Red as a nickname has usually been associated with the colour of hair, like Frederick I, German king and Roman emperor, known as 'Barbarossa' because of his red beard; and there was Napoleon's marshal Ney, called '*le Rougeaud*' because his hair was a chestnut colour.)

S

sabbatarians: the original name for Jews who strictly observe the seventh day of the week as sacred, and for early Christians similarly who recognised the seventh day as such in addition to Sunday; conveniently extended to those with an uncompromising adherence to the Christian Sunday as a day of rest. Two periods in English history when sabbatarianism was particularly marked were during the seventeenth-century commonwealth and the second half of Victoria's reign. The Lord's Day Observance Society has for long been active. See *puritan Sunday.*

sabbatical leave: a 'grace and favour' holiday granted to members of staff, usually in recognition of long service, or for some special period of travel and study. The term not only originates in the Jewish and Christian observance of the sabbath as a day of rest and given over to religious devotion, but also from the 'sabbatical year' of the ancient Hebrews— every seventh year—when this agricultural people allowed the fields to go unsown, the vines unpruned (although not all of a person's land may have been left fallow). Another edict, according to *Exodus* xxiii, was that when the land was un-cultivated every seventh year the crop it yielded—including grapes and olives—should be left to the poor, 'and what they leave the wild beasts may eat'.

Sacheverell affair, the: a sensation in 1709–10 when Dr Henry Sacheverell (c1674–1724) preached at Derby and then at St Paul's before the lord mayor of London, supporting the church and criticising the whig ministry, sermons which were printed and which led to his impeachment. His trial at Westminster Hall lasted more than three weeks, and queen Anne attended. He was found guilty and suspended from office for three years, his pamphlets to be burned at the Royal Exchange. Tory-whig feeling was running high among the public, and Sacheverell was regarded as something of a martyr. There were riots and dissenters' chapels were burned down. The whig ministry fell.

sailor king, the: William IV (1765–1837), a nickname he enjoyed, because he had long wished—as duke of Clarence, and as a midshipman and then a captain before that—to have his services to the navy recognised. As duke he had fretted about inactivity, not being given a command, and was delighted when—on the death of the duke of York in 1827 and he became heir to the throne—he was appointed lord high admiral. Because of his interference in naval affairs, however, he was asked to resign.

St Martin's summer: see *Indian summer*.

St Monday: a jocular reference to workmen taking a day off, lengthening the week-end and observing Monday as if it were a 'holy day', a holiday, a saint's day.

sally army: the Salvation Army.

sally-lunn: a sweet tea-cake as sold by Sally Lunn, a pastry-cook, in the streets of Bath around 1800. They are recommended to be buttered and eaten warm.

SALT: Strategic Arms Limitation Talks, the post-Second World War periodic conferences between heads of states to obtain agreement on weapon manufacture, especially nuclear.

Sam: see *uncle Sam*.

sam browne: an army issue leather belt with a strap attached and going over the right shoulder, named after general Sir S. Browne (1824–1901) who introduced it.

Sandemanians: people who left the church of Scotland to follow John Glas (1695–1773) who maintained that national churches such as those of Scotland and England were contrary to scripture, and who criticised church government to the extent of repudiating Presbyterianism. He was joined by Robert Sandeman who became his son-in-law and leader of the movement, introducing strict doctrines according to his views of primitive Christianity. The movement (whose members were generally known in Scotland as Glasites) spread to England and America. Glas introduced the kiss of peace, and the love feast, celebrated as a common meal with broth, from which custom the congregation was known in Scotland as 'the kail kirk'.

sandwich: originally the nickname for two slices of bread with meat between them, as prepared for the convenience of the fourth earl of Sandwich (1718–92) so that he need not interrupt his card-playing for a meal. It became a recognised word and extended to a verb meaning to insert or compress. But Lord Sandwich is commemorated in other ways: see *Jemmy Twitcher*.

Satchmo: (contraction of 'satchelmouth'), Louis (Daniel) Armstrong (1900–71), jazz trumpeter and singer, leader of dance orchestras and world famous for his influence on jazz music and his unique style of improvisation. He was also called 'Pops'.

Saxon shore, the: east coast of England from the Wash south, and the south coast to the Isle of Wight, named either because of their vulnerability to Saxon attack or because the invaders built settlements in these regions. Forts and other defences were unified by a count of the Saxon shore in the fourth century.

scarlet woman: a harlot; used as an abusive nickname by early protestants for the Roman catholic church, selecting a passage from *Revelation* xvii. See *whore of Babylon*.

Sealed Knot, the: a royalist society formed after the civil wars to work against Cromwell and for the restoration of monarchy.

seamy side, the: unpleasant aspects of life, the hidden places where poverty and perhaps crime abound. The reference is to the underside of garments and cloths where the seams are stitched, the rough work beneath the smarter surface.

seekers: groups of seventeenth-century dissenters who rejected formalities of worship and laid stress on silent prayer and 'waiting upon God'. They were loosely connected by itinerant preachers, and it was from among them that George Fox got some of his followers in the early years of Quakerism.

sex kitten, the: entertainment columnists' tribute to Brigitte Bardot (b. 1934), French film actress.

sexy sixties: a journalistic identification of the nineteen-sixties when there was a marked change in moral attitudes and behaviour, and a publicly-expressed emphasis on sexual relationships, young people living together out of wedlock, concern for the unmarried mother, stories of 'wife swapping', an upsurge of 'girlie' magazines with nude pictures, and frank revelations in readers' correspondence columns of intimate marital problems, and a relaxation of taboos in films and on television. It was the decade of the topless dress, the rise (literally) of the mini-skirt, and the introduction of 'the pill' q.v. contraceptive.

Many decades have had their packaged identification; cf. the 'naughty nineties' q.v., the 'roaring twenties' q.v., and the 'years of crises' in the nineteen-thirties. Social historians may one day dub the nineteen-seventies as the 'striking seventies' because of the large number of industrial disputes and the domination of the country by trade unions, something new. But other characteristics are not new. Boswell in his *Life of Johnson*, for example, records general Paoli's asking what the doctor thought of the spirit of infidelity then prevalent (1769), to which Johnson replied that it was 'only a transient cloud passing through the hemisphere'.

shadow cabinet: name popularised from 1964 for the opposition counterparts to the government ministers in office, specialising in their particular subjects.

Shakers: a religious community started in Manchester, 1747, by James and Jane Wardley (formerly Quakers) and nick-named thus because of their emotional form of worship which led them to be wrongly described as 'shaking Quakers'. The Wardleys were succeeded by Ann Lee (1736–84), a former factory worker and cook, several times imprisoned for breaking the sabbath by dancing and shouting, and for blasphemy. 'Mother Lee', or 'Ann the Word', as she was called, argued for celibacy (although herself married), temperance and communal living, sharing all possessions. In 1774 she led the sect to America where communities were established in New York, Massachusetts, Connecticut and elsewhere. Their craftsmanship in woodwork and weaving (non-profit making enteprises), their honesty and orderliness, won admiration, and their spiritual communism attracted attention.

shank's mare: walking, using one's shanks.

shop, the: Royal Military Academy, formerly at Woolwich.

shrieking sisterhood, the: nickname given by their detractors and current between 1908 and 1914 for the suffragettes q.v. because of their shouted slogans and their sometimes high-pitched harangues at public meetings, especially outdoors.

silly Billy: William Frederick, duke of Gloucester, cousin of William IV to whom the nickname has also been given, but the duke earned it first. In the wrangles between whigs and tories, when the king supported the former, Gloucester is reported to have asked, 'Who is silly Billy now?' (Quoted by Philip Ziegler, *King William IV*, London, Collins, 1971.)

silly season: a journalistic term which began to lose its use and meaning after the Second World War as social conditions changed and world and national events competed for coverage. Originally it meant the summer period when the London social season ended, parliament was in recess and public affairs were interrupted by holidays, so that newspapers 'blew up' trivial stories and searched for unusual tit-bits to fill the space normally occupied by 'hard' news. 'Silly' items found a market—the longest leek at the produce show, the man who claimed to have the ugliest face, the horse that drank beer, etc.

Simon pure: a hypocrite, one who makes a display of virtue, from a character in *A Bold Stroke for a Wife*, 1718, by Susannah Centlivre (1667–1723). She was an actress as well as dramatist and used her married name, S. Carroll. In her play a suitor pretends he is a Quaker called Simon Pure to gain the consent of a girl's guardian, but the real Simon turns up in time.

Sinbad the tailor: Emmanuel (to become Lord) Shinwell, when he was a rising young trade unionist and efficient agitator at the beginning of the century. The press gave him this ephemeral nickname when, as representative of the garment workers in Glasgow he also helped to organise a seamen's strike.

Sir Reverse: a nickname given in the early part of the Boer War to general Sir Redvers Henry Buller (1839–1908), a distinguished soldier who had won the VC in the Zulu War but when in command of the campaign in South Africa he was no match for the Boers, and his army suffered reverses at Colenso and Spion Kop. He was replaced by Lord Roberts, nicknamed 'Bobs' q.v.

sitzkreig: joking reference to the comparatively quiet few months on the home front at the beginning of the Second World War, 1939, compared with the 'blitz' q.v. that Hitler had been waging across the channel. It was only a short period of 'sitting' and waiting. It was also absurdly called 'the phoney war'.

sixteen-string Jack: John Rann, a highwayman, hanged in 1774. His victims noted that he wore eight tags to his trousers on each knee.

sky pilot: a forces' nickname for a padre in the First World War, rarely used in the Second.

skyscraper: American description of a towering multi-storey building, adopted in Britain.

slapstick: showbusiness name for broad, knockabout comedy, the word recalling the original pantomime when Harlequin or the clown wielded two light laths, fastened together at one end, so that when a blow was struck the sound was loud from the pieces of wood hitting each other. This was the 'slapstick'.

sleeping partner: the member of a board or firm who takes no active part: he may have supplied his name, advice or capital.

smoke, the (or the big smoke): London, because of its one-time contaminated atmosphere from its many chimneys. John Evelyn was complaining about London's pall of smoke as early as 1661, and he wrote a pamphlet—*Fumifugium*—urging restrictions. Charles II showed great interest. Byron described the city, *Don Juan* x as 'A mighty mass of brick, and smoke, and shipping'; and in another poem (*Italy*) is his line, 'Where reeking London's smoky caldron simmers.' In a letter to Bulwer Lytton in 1851, Dickens wrote: 'London is a vile place . . . Whenever I come back from the country now, and see the great heavy canopy lowering over the house-tops, I wonder what I'd do there except on obligation.' (Quoted by Angus Wilson, *The World of Charles Dickens*, London, Secker and Warburg, 1970.) The nickname became a slangword, especially used by criminals in fact and fiction—'escaping to the smoke'. Cf. *Auld Reekie* q.v.

snake, the: system within the European Economic Community ('common market' q.v.) for regulating the limits of rise and fall of currencies—the up and down movements in relation to each other as shown on a graph. The term came into general use early in 1976 when the pound was under great pressure.

soap opera: trivial, undemanding entertainment, of the kind devised to allow breaks for advertising (soap, cosmetics, etc.) on commercial radio and television; extended to refer to long-running serials. Another Americanism which found favour in Britain.

soapy Sam: Samuel Wilberforce (1805–73), bishop of Oxford, later of Winchester, a man of determination and a powerful preacher, persuasive in argument, earning the nickname because of his efforts to smooth things over between men of opposing points of view. He was noted for his wit, and his own explanation of the nickname was that he often got into hot water but emerged with clean hands.

sob sister: a journalist who answers readers' questions, dealing with intimate problems, allowing the writers to weep on her shoulder. The term is an American invention, but such an adviser had long been known in British ladies' magazines, the subjects usually confined to household management and points of etiquette, but developing with popular journalism into those of wider—and more personal—interests. Such columnists achieved high standing in post-Second World War years, none with greater distinction than Marjorie Proops of the *Daily Mirror*, a trusted confidante. In a profile of her in *The Observer*, 4 May, 1975, her advice was described as 'startlingly good, entertaining and sensible', adding: 'Her skill is that she is a campaigner. She isn't one of those passive sob sisters who field each letter that comes as best they can . . .'

sociable: an open horse-drawn carriage, so dubbed because it had side seats facing each other; also, and for a similar reason, a tricycle with two seats side by side; both nineteenth century.

software: information programmed into a computer, the 'hardware' q.v.

sons of the soil: farm labourers, land workers of various kinds.

sons of thunder: nickname given by Jesus to James and John —'whom he surnamed Boanerges, that is, sons of thunder': *Mark* iii.

Southcottians: followers of Joanna Southcott (1750–1814), religious eccentric, former domestic servant who began to prophesy, and who announced that she would give birth to a second Christ at the age of sixty-four. She gave the exact date, and died ten days later. She left a box, to be opened in time of national crisis in the presence of all the bishops. It purported to contain miraculous documents, but when opened in 1927 it was found to hold trivial oddments and a lottery ticket.

southpaw: a boxer who leads with his right hand.

south sea bubble: a series of financial schemes, beginning with the formation of the South Sea Company in 1711—with a monopoly of trade with south America and the Pacific islands in return for taking over a large part of the national debt—and collapsing in 1720 after an epidemic of speculation when hundreds of imitative companies had been launched and £100 shares were fetching as much as £1,100. Some of the companies, taking advantage of the get-rich-quick mania, promoted fantastic schemes. The South Sea Company prospered for some years, but when stock fell and everybody was a seller thousands of people were ruined.

spencer: a short overcoat or jacket, as supplied to the second earl Spencer (1758–1834). Several items have been named 'spencer', including a man's wig and a woman's bodice.

spiv: one who lives on his wits, making money without really working, usually nattily dressed as he goes about his business: 'a relentless opportunist, a picker-up of considerable as well as of unconsidered trifles', as Eric Partridge defines him in an essay in *Here There and Everywhere*, London, Hamish Hamilton, 1950. The origin of the word is obscure: late in the nineteenth century it was used for a bookmaker's runner: during the earlier part of the twentieth it was identified with a smart and non-violent operator on the fringe of actual crime, coming into his own in wartime and post-war rationing 'black markets' q.v.

sport of kings, the: horse racing, because of royal patronage, dating at least as far back as Charles II whose stables at Newmarket were among his great interests.

squarson: a combination of 'squire' and 'parson', as were so many incumbents in eighteenth- and nineteenth-century England. 'Sabine Baring-Gould was rector—more accurately, squarson—of Lew Trenchard in Devon': Piers Brandon, *Hawker of Norwenstow*, London, Cape, 1975 (in the foreword by John Fowles).

stanhope: a light open carriage with two or four wheels, according to *SOED* first made for the hon and rev Fitzroy Stanhope (1787–1864). 'The streets in the West End in the season were crowded with elegant carriages: stanhopes as high as a first-floor window . . .': Stella Margetson, *Regency London*, London, Cassell, 1971.

star chamber: a room in the palace of Westminster where sat the king's council and judges, a court of civil and criminal jurisdiction, so called because the ceiling was decorated with painted stars. Established in 1487, it was abolished in 1641. The name became synonymous with tyrannical procedure.

stars and stripes: flag of the USA, the alternating red and white horizontal bars representing the original thirteen states, the stars the states in the union, a pattern laid down in 1818 after several designs following the declaration of independence. The number of stars increased as other states joined the union. 'Stars and bars' was the nickname given to the flag of the confederate states which broke away from the union in 1861: it had two horizontal red bars on white, and a circle with eleven white stars on a blue background. 'Old glory' is another nickname for the national flag, also 'the star spangled banner' used in the national song composed by Francis Scott Key:

Oh say, does the star-spangled banner yet wave
O'er the land of the free and the home of the brave?

And there was John Philip Sousa's 'Stars and Stripes for Ever'.

Steenie: George Villiers, first duke of Buckingham (1592–1628), favourite of James I who gave him high honours and this nickname, alluding to Stephen (*Acts* vi) who was 'full of grace' and people 'saw that his face was like the face of an angel'. Villiers's youthful charm delighted the king, but as his power and influence grew—he was for a time virtually ruler of England—he undertook more than he could accomplish in foreign affairs. Parliament attacked him, and a man with a grievance stabbed him to death.

strad: a violin made by Antonio Stradivari (c1644–1737), perhaps the greatest craftsman in this field, or in his workshop. See *cremona*.

street arabs: Victorian name for poor boys, wandering (like Arabs) in the streets. They earned a few pennies by sweeping street crossings: they begged, and their wanderings led them into petty crime. See also *mud-larks*.

strongbow: Richard de Clare, second earl of Pembroke, who succeeded to his father's estates in 1148, did much fighting in Ireland and was beloved by his soldiers who gave him this nickname. He was tall and fair, courteous and wise, as well as being a man of valour.

submerged tenth: the poorer, unnoticed people, an appellation given by William Booth (1829–1912), founder of the Salvation Army, to the destitutes and unemployables.

subtopia: suburban housing estates, each householder striving to make the best of his small plot, probably the house and garden being the culmination of his ambitions: a word coined by architectural journalist Ian Nairn in the nineteen-fifties.

suburbia: a description in use in the eighteen-nineties for London's expanding suburbs. 'If you walk down the Clapham Road, from the end of the Common to Clapham Road Station, with your eyes open, you will have seen the best part of all that Suburbia has to show you': quotation from *The Suburbans* (1905) by Donald Read, *Edwardian England*, London, Harrap, 1972. The growth of suburbia in big towns and cities marked a social stratification from mid-Victorian times: while the lower (working) classes lived in old, near-slum conditions, the lower middle classes occupied the inner suburbs, and the middle-and-upper middle classes moved to outer suburbs and further afield.

suffragettes: nickname generally accepted (others like 'the shrieking sisterhood' q.v. were vituperative and transient) for members of the movement demanding votes for women, waging a campaign of oratory, petitions, demonstrations and militancy which eventually succeeded. Mrs Emmeline Pankhurst and her husband founded the Women's Franchise League in 1889, and in 1903 she formed the Women's Social and Political Union. She and her daughters, Christabel and Sylvia, worked tirelessly with others against all opposition. Militancy began in 1905 when Christabel and Annie Kenney were thrown out of Manchester's Free Trade Hall, continued their protest in the street, were arrested and sent to prison. A plaque in the hall commemorates the event. Their fighting colours were purple, white and green. See *women's lib.*

sunny Jim: Leonard James Callaghan MP, cabinet minister in Labour administrations, smiling in the face of adversity and earning himself this journalistic tag. While foreign secretary a profile of him in *The Observer*, 8 June, 1975, was headed: 'Assets of Sunny Jim'. He became prime minister, 1976.

supermac: Harold Macmillan, Conservative MP and prime minister, 1957–63. In his long and distinguished career he had been minister of defence, foreign secretary and chancellor of the exchequer. The nickname was created by the political cartoonist Vicky in 1958. See *Mac the knife*.

swan of Avon: William Shakespeare, born at Stratford-on-Avon 1564, one of several honorifics.

swan of Lichfield: Anna Seward (1747–1809), poet and author, admired and visited by Dr Johnson in his home town of Lichfield where she lived. She in return admired him to adulation. Later Sir Walter Scott edited her poetical works.

Swedenborgians: followers of Emmanuel Swedenborg (1688–1772), Swedish philosopher and mystic who abandoned scientific work for study and to propound his theories on the relationship between the physical and spiritual world. He was remarkably inventive, with great scientific skill and imagination, but in 1747 his life took an entirely new direction after what he claimed to be a directive from God. He died in London.

Swedish nightingale, the: Jenny (Johanna Maria) Lind (1820–87), whose great talents as a singer made her famous in Europe (especially Germany and Britain) and in America. She excelled in opera and Handel's *Messiah*. England was her home in the latter part of her life, and she died at Malvern.

T

tail-end Charlie: RAF nickname for the rear gunner in a bomber: also the last in a flight of 'planes.

tails: short for swallow-tails, descriptive of the shape of the male formal evening dress coat, worn with white shirt and white tie; also used for the whole black-and-white ensemble.

talkies: talking pictures when they were introduced into the cinema in the late nineteen-twenties, an Americanism quickly adopted in Britain. Experiments with short sound films had been taking place for several years, and in 1926 there was a spectacular showing of *Don Juan* with synchronised music recorded by the New York Philharmonic Orchestra. Then in October, 1927, came the first spoken words from the screen—Al Jolson in *The Jazz Singer* at the Warner Theatre, New York. The first all-talking feature was *Lights of New York*, followed by Jolson in *The Singing Fool* which, although not 'all talking', was a sensational success. Cinemas rapidly became 'wired for sound'.

talking heads: a television producer's term for discussion programmes.

tallyman: salesman (as a hawker or shopkeeper) who provided goods on credit, paid for by installments, thus the nickname from the tally, meaning a notch (French, *taille*), going back to the fifteenth century. The tally was a stick with notches cut on it to record transactions, hence 'tally-shop' and 'tally' meaning to correspond with, to duplicate—the salesman and customer checking their notches.

tam o' shanter: a round wollen cap as worn by Scottish ploughmen, from the man in Burns's poem of that name, 1789; sometimes called tammy shanter. It was introduced as a fashionable cap or bonnet around 1840.

tantalus: unkind nickname, with domestic servants in mind, for the stand of spirit decanters secured by a locked frame for which the master had the key; so aptly conceived that it quickly became a proper description. Tantalus, son of Zeus in Greek mythology, was condemned to stand in hades with water and fruit within reach but always receding when he tried to get at them. Tantalising indeed!

tantivy: derisory nickname for high churchmen at the time of James II's support for Roman catholics, based on a caricature of such clergymen mounted on the church of England and 'riding tantivy' (that is, at a gallop) to Rome.

teach-in: an Americanism adopted in Britain from the nineteen-sixties to describe a meeting or a series of lectures and discussions on a particular subject.

teddy boys: youths who adopted Edwardian style of dress in the nineteen-fifties and behaved bullyingly and violently, clashing with the public and police; elegant in appearance, anti-social in outlook; smarter precursors of 'hell's angels' who took to leather jackets and motor-bikes, and 'mods and rockers' q.v.

Telstar: see *Early Bird*.

think tank: accepted nickname for the Central Policy Review Staff, initiated under the premiership of Edward Heath (1970–4) and retained by succeeding governments. 'Mr Wilson and his senior colleagues have ordered a major review of Britain's Foreign Service, to be carried out by Sir Kenneth Berrill and his staff at the "Think Tank" in the Cabinet office . . .': *The Guardian*, 15 January, 1976.

thin red line, the: a description of the 93rd Highlanders at the battle of Balaclava, invented by William Howard Russell when special correspondent of *The Times* covering the Crimean war. The phrase so caught the public imagination that it was transferred to British soldiers generally who faced an enemy charge, bayonets fixed, a stubborn line of opposition in scarlet coats. As in Kipling's poem 'Tommy' (*Barrack Room Ballads*): 'But it's "Thin red line of 'eroes" when the drums begin to roll.' Russell (1820–1907) was one of the earliest— and finest—war correspondents. He covered the Indian mutiny, the civil war in America, and the Franco-Prussian war. He was knighted in 1895. See John Selby *The Thin Red Line*, Hamish Hamilton, 1970.

third world, the: poorer, less developed countries (mostly in Africa, and also parts of Asia) than those on the American continent and in Europe, a term invented after the Second World War. A typical headline: 'Third World hit by price of oil', *The Guardian*, 12 March, 1975. 'We have grown a spiritual carapace to protect ourselves against the pictures and descriptions of distress in the Third World which otherwise would make excessive demands on our ability to feel sympathy', *The Common Catechism*, London, Search Press, 1975.

Thomas the rhymer: Thomas of Erceldoune in Scotland, sometimes given the surname of Learmont. He lived in the thirteenth century and has a place in Scottish legend as a poet and a prophet.

three-decker: (1) a warship with three gun-decks in the days of wooden vessels when 'Hearts of oak are our ships . . .'; (2) the high eighteenth-century pulpit with three positions, the clerk's desk at the bottom, reading desk in the middle, and the topmost being a pulpit for the clergyman giving his sermon; (3) the nineteenth-century three-volume novel. 'When the immense popularity of the works of Sir Walter Scott had forced up the price of newly-published novels to a guinea and a half for the customary three volumes . . . with three-deckers at 31/6—a price sustained still to make borrowers feel they were getting value for their subscription—the libraries had been omnipotent . . .' Alan Walbank, *Queens of the Circulating Library*, London, Evans Brothers, 1950.

Throgmorton street: London's boastful nickname for the financial world, centred on the stock exchange there, but the term had fallen out of general currency by the nineteen-thirties. Cf. *the city*, and *old lady of Threadneedle street*, both q.v.

thunderer, the: Edward Sterling (1773–1847) who, under the pseudonym of Vetus, wrote vigorous letters to *The Times* which were re-printed, and in 1915 he joined the staff and became virtual editor under Thomas Barnes, continuing his robust and crusading style, with such expressions as 'We thundered forth the other day . . .' The nickname conferred on him was quickly transferred to the paper itself, so that *The Times* became 'the thunderer'.

tich: a little man, from the popular music-hall comedian Harry Relph (1868–1928) who performed under the name of Little Tich. This was his own nickname, probably invented by his family, because when he was a baby the sensational Tichborne case was still attracting argument—the claim made in 1866 by a man from Australia that he was the missing heir to a Hampshire baronetcy and fortune. The claimant

156

(Arthur Orton), who was imprisoned for perjury, was plump —as no doubt was Harry Relph as a little boy, and who remained small in stature and used the nickname to good purpose.

tiger, the: Georges Clemenceau (1841–1929), French statesman, so called when he toppled several ministries after 1876. As a member of the chamber and as prime minister he introduced many reforms, and the nickname clung to him with special significance during the First World War.

tilbury: an open two-wheeled horse-drawn carriage named after the London firm of coachbuilders which designed it.

timwhisky: a high light carriage, pulled by one or a pair of horses, the word probably denoting the dash and liveliness of the equipage and driver.

tin Lizzie: Henry Ford's famous 'model T' motor-car, the first mass-produced vehicle, efficient if inelegant, and comparatively cheap, so that fifteen million were produced between 1908 and the discontinuation of the model in 1927. These all-black cars rattled round the world, and were sturdy and popular. Mr Ford is said to have encouraged the jokes that were made about them: all good for publicity.

tin pan alley: popular music and those who compose, perform and publish it, from the nickname given from the eighteen-nineties to a street off Times Square, New York, identified with the tinkle of pianos (some professed to think it sounded like the rattle of tin pans). The name came over the Atlantic to the Charing Cross road district of London, especially Denmark street.

tippling house: originally an innocuous enough nickname for a tavern, where beer was poured by a 'tippler', that is, a publican. *ODEE* traces the word to the fourteenth century. Out of it, about two hundred years later, a new meaning had developed for 'tippler', one who is an habitual drinker—not the publican who tipples the beer into the mug but the customer who pours liquor down his own throat.

toad-eater: the assistant, usually a boy, accompanying a 'quack' q.v. doctor around eighteenth-century villages, named

157

thus because that was exactly what he did—or pretended to do—eat a toad (believed to be poisonous) at the command of his master whose nostrum warded-off any ill effects. Hence, an obsequious person, doing anything to please; a toady.

Tokyo Rose: name given by US servicemen to the girl whose voice broadcasting to them on Japanese radio in the Second World War told them they were sacrificing home comforts in a futile fight against invincible forces. Cf. similar propaganda by 'Lord Haw-haw' q.v. to British civilians and servicemen on the Germans' behalf.

Tolpuddle martyrs, the: six farm labourers from the Dorsetshire village of Tolpuddle who formed a union to improve their conditions and were sentenced to transportation to Australia in 1834 on a charge of administering illegal oaths. The government at that time was concerned about working class unrest. There was a public outcry and demonstrations on the Tolpuddle men's behalf, and they were pardoned two years later.

Tom, Dick and Harry: every ordinary man (these being common names); a Victorian expression which has persisted for the 'man-in-the-street' q.v.

tom-fool: an idiotic kind of fellow, often up to pranks, at least as old as the sixteenth century, one of several nicknames incorporating Tom, the diminutive of Thomas which has always been a common Christian name: cf. 'tom-noddy', a feckless person or a blockhead, and 'tom-cat', a male of the feline species.

Tommy (Atkins): the British 'other ranks' soldier, from the specimen signature of Thomas Atkins on attestation forms and other documents. (I have not been able to find which nineteenth-century military man or civil servant can be credited with this historic choice of a hypothetical name.) 'Tommy' spread throughout the empire and the world as the nickname for the ordinary British soldier:

O it's Tommy this, an' Tommy that, an' 'Tommy, go away';
But it's 'Thank you, Mister Atkins', when the band begins to play

Kipling, *Barrack Room Ballads*, 1892

Cf. Jack tar, John Doe, both q.v.

tommy-gun: the Thompson sub-machine gun, much used as a personal quick-fire weapon in the Second World War.

Tom o' Bedlam: a beggar, pleading insanity. See *Abraham men.*

Tom Thumb: Charles Sherwood Stratton (1838–83), an American dwarf who was dubbed 'general' Tom Thumb when he toured with P. T. Barnum's show. He was only about two feet high when first exhibited, but he grew to about three feet four inches, and in 1863 he married another dwarf called Lavinia. He and his wife were received by president Lincoln, and by queen Victoria when they came to England. The nickname came from very old fairy tales, the hero being only the size of a thumb.

tories: an abusive nickname for Irish Roman catholics, and formerly for the dispossessed Irish of the sixteenth and seventeenth centuries who became outlaws and attacked English settlers and soldiers, from an Irish word meaning 'pursuit'. The word has had a chequered history, being transferred as a nickname for militant Irish catholics to those Englishmen who opposed the exclusion of the duke of York from the throne as James II (he was a Roman catholic), and hence to the political party that was formed in the cavalier tradition. Towards the end of the seventeenth century the opposing political ideologies were lined up as whigs and tories, the supporters of each flinging nicknames at each other, because 'whig' q.v. is also a nickname. It is yet another example of a sneering nickname being absorbed as a respectable word, although 'whigs' has faded from use whereas 'tories' is retained as a convenient alternative to the 'Conservative' party which took its title under Peel and Disraeli.

town and gown: the citizens and local government of a town in which a university—represented by academic gowns—is situated.

toyshop of Europe: Birmingham, as much for its export of nicknacks and trinkets as for its toys in Victorian and Edwardian times: as well as its many great industries, the Birmingham district has for long been associated with cheap jewellery.

159

tractarians: members of the Oxford movement, q.v., because of the many *Tracts for the Times* initiated in 1833 by John Henry (later cardinal, when he had joined the Roman Catholic church) Newman, the object being to find a definite basis of doctrine and discipline for the Church of England.

Traskites: followers of John Trask, a seventeenth-century evangelist who argued for the strict observance of the sabbath and the literal interpretation of the Old Testament. He made a nuisance of himself and was stood in the pillory.

travellers (or travelling people, the): gipsies.

trencher cap: the college cap, likening it to an inverted basin on a trencher (that is, a wooden plate). There is an interesting connection with the zuchetto (now an English dictionary word), the skull-cap of a Roman ecclesiastic which covers the tonsure. *ODEE* traces the origin to the Italian *zuchetta*, a small gourd as well as a cap, the diminutive of *zucca*, a gourd. (This explanation should be read along with that for 'mortar board' q.v.)

trencher knight: one who likes his food, who concentrates on his trencher (plate, originally of wood and all-purpose for food: now used only for a bread-board). Such a man was valiant for meals. 'Some mumble-news, some trencher knight, some Dick', says Berowne in *Love's Labour's Lost* (V. ii). The nickname has lingered in the language in the form of trencherman for a 'good' eater, a glutton.

tricky Dickie: Richard Milhous Nixon, elected president of the USA, 1969, and then for a second term. He resigned in August, 1974, after the 'Watergate' q.v. scandal. Despite his many achievements, journalists on both sides of the Atlantic adopted the nickname to indicate his art of manipulation and evasion.

trilby: a soft black felt hat, named after the novel of that title by George du Maurier, 1894. In the stage version Beerbohm Tree wore such a hat, although more flamboyant than the later men's fashion, in the part of Svengali, the sinister influence on the artists' model, Trilby.

truce of God, the: a halt in hostilities in medieval times when feudal lords fought their neighbours—and further afield—disrupting normal life. It was decreed that fighting should cease during church festivals, such as Lent and Advent; also between noon on Saturday and Monday morning—a quiet week-end. There were various edicts, going back to the tenth century, beginning with the *pax ecclesiae* in France, intended to protect non-combatants and church property, and then the prohibition of private warfare on certain days under the *treva Dei*. The general term of *pax Dei* was incorporated into church and royal laws, but does not seem to have been long effective in England.

tube, the: London underground railways, so familiar a name that it is difficult to realise that it began as nickname before 1890. J. H. Greathead in 1886 started building the City and South London railway under the Thames, using the shield method of construction (invented in principle by Brunel) to cut a circular tunnel—the 'tube'—and making it possible for trains to run safely many feet below the surface of the ground.

tumbledown Dick: Richard Cromwell (1626–1712), Oliver's son, who tumbled after a short and ineffectual reign as protector. See *queen Dick*.

turf, the: horse racing and all those connected with it, including the 'turf account', a bookmaker.

turncoat: nickname for one who changes his allegiance, turning the colour or cut of his coat to suit the prevailing political fashion, like the legendary vicar of Bray; one who goes over to the other side.

turnip: a nineteenth century bulbous gold watch.

turnip hoer, the: George I (1660–1727) who was said to have suggested turning St James's park, London, into a turnip field.

Twiggy: nickname that became the professional name for Lesley Hornby, slim London girl, whose distinctive personality brought her fame as a model in the nineteen-sixties, her talents later taking her to a stage and television career as singer and dancer.

twin, the: the apostle Thomas, 'called the twin' (*John* xi). John in the gospel refers to the translation of the Aramaic name into the Greek Didymus, meaning twin. There is much confusion in the name, as there is in Thomas's antecedants, one tradition being that he had a twin sister, another that his full name was Judas Thomas and that he may have been a brother of Jesus himself. See *doubting Thomas*.

two cultures, the: the humanities and the sciences, a term popularised by the writer C. P. (Lord) Snow in 1959, posing the problem of the lack of contact between the two. Lord Snow, novelist and writer on sociological and educational subjects, was himself a scientist in his early career.

U

U and non-U: distinction between the social classes, especially in the use of words which betray their upbringings, a pleasantry introduced by writer Nancy Mitford in 1955 in an article in the magazine *Encounter*, inspired by an essay on the subject of sociological linguistics by the philologist professor Alan S. C. Ross (Birmingham University). Miss Mitford's article sparked off an amusing response from writers and the public, with accusations of snobbery. There followed a book, *Noblesse Oblige*, London, Hamish Hamilton, 1956, to which Miss Mitford, professor Ross, Evelyn Waugh, John Betjeman and other contributed. The U people (upper class) would naturally say 'table napkin', for example, while their social inferiors would use the word 'serviette'; and the U's would say 'lavatory' for what the non-U's, aspiring to gentility, would call 'the toilet'.

U-boat: name given to the German submarine, the *untersee-boot*, in two world wars.

UFO's: unidentified flying objects. See *flying saucers*.

ugly duckling: the less-favoured (in looks) member of a family; someone of unprepossessing appearance who may change into something attractive, as in Hans Andersen's story of that name; extended to signify a rejected person.

uncle: a pawnbroker, from mid-eighteenth century, a convenient and euphemistic nickname, suggestive of the helpful relative to whom one can turn in time of trouble.

uncle Joe: Joseph V. Stalin (1879–1953), when he was people's commissar for the defence of the USSR, 1941–6, and later president of the Soviet council of ministers; a newspaper nickname.

uncle Paul: Paul (or Paulus) Kruger (1825–1904), four times elected president of the Transvaal republic, an 'uncle' if not 'father' figure in his own domain and in South Africa generally, although his political career was controversial. His aim was the domination of South Africa by the Boers, and the nickname was current during the Boer (or South African) War.

uncle Sam: personification of the USA as John Bull q.v. is of England. The name has been used since early in the nineteenth century, most likely an invention from the initials US on government supplies to the forces. Cf. GI's q.v.

uncrowned king of Ireland, the: Charles Stewart Parnell (1846–91), Irish politician, leader of the Irish party in the house of commons and a valiant fighter for home rule. His extremely active and distinguished career was blighted when he was cited as co-respondent in a divorce case: he married the lady, Mrs O'Shea, in 1891.

union jack: beginning as a nickname (Jack for James—Jacobus, or Jacques as James I usually signed himself) for the British flag when the red cross of St George for England was joined under James I (1603) with the diagonal white cross-on-blue of St Andrew for Scotland, and then in 1801 with the diagonal red-on-white cross of St Patrick for Ireland.

unisex: a casual fashion adopted by young people from the nineteen-sixties of shirt and jeans for both sexes, so that—boys wearing their hair long—it was often difficult to distinguish male from female.

unmentionables: used first euphemistically for men's trousers, then for women's underwear: origin obscure, like the undergarments (usually female) which the word began to refer to; a delicate reference to what were once called 'underpinnings'. Cf. 'inexpressibles' q.v.

163

unready, the: see *Ethelred the unready*.

unwashed: see *great unwashed*.

upper house, the: house of lords.

upper ten: short for upper ten thousand, the higher echelons of society, thought to have been coined for the elite of New York by Nathaniel Parker Willis (1806–67), American author and journalist who spent much time in England and several of his books were published here.

V

vamp: a flirtatious woman whose charms entrap the male, jocularly suggestive of the legendary vampire which sucks the blood of its victim. It was a term much in vogue in the silent film days for a type of 'get her man' heroine who used her sexual attractions without stint. 'The innocent heroine of the serial was soon supplanted in public favor by the "vamp", and the film gained in sophistication what it lost in simple morality. Billed as the "wickedest face in the world", Theda Bara not only symbolized this new siren, she played her to the hilt': Frederic Thrasher, *Okay for Sound*, New York, Duell, Sloan and Pearce, 1946.

vandyke: a collar or cape slit into points, and any one of these points forming a border to lace and linen neck-bands, as worn in the portraits by Sir Anthony Van Dyck (1599–1641), the Flemish artist who became court painter to Charles I. (His name was anglicised for the purpose of the word.) It also became descriptive of the small pointed beard such as those of most of his male sitters, including the king himself. A less-familiar nickname for such a beard was a 'charlie'.

VE day: victory in Europe day, 8 May, 1945.

velveteens: mid-Victorian nickname for a gamekeeper, because so many on the large estates wore jackets (and perhaps trousers) of this fabric, closely-woven cotton with a velvet pile; also an appropriate name because the furry covering over the growing antlers of a deer is called velvet.

vesta: a wax friction match, given the name from Vesta, the Greek goddess of the hearth, the family fire, and at whose temple the virgin priestesses officiated and kept the sacred fire burning.

vicar of hell: two people seem to have carried this nickname in the reign of Henry VIII—John Skelton (c1460–1529), who had been tutor to Henry when he was a young prince and became rector of Diss in Norfolk, and poet laureate; and Sir Francis Bryan, a favourite at court who took the news of Anne Boleyn's condemnation to Jane Seymour, Henry's future wife. Bryan had some hand in his cousin Anne's downfall. King Henry playfully gave Skelton the nickname, punning on the word Diss, an old alternative for Pluto, god of the lower regions, and Skelton's satirical verses and the scandals credited to him strengthened the reference. Thomas Cromwell, chamberlain to Henry, is said to have given Bryan the nickname: the reason is obscure.

VIP (vee-aye-pee): convenient initials used in instructions to service chiefs in the Second World War, warning them of a visit from 'very important person(s)', and retained in the language; used in expressions such as 'VIP treatment' and 'fit for a VIP'.

virgin queen, the: Elizabeth I (1533–1603), one of the many adulatory epithets bestowed on her, although how virginal she was is questionable, despite her never marrying or producing children. Another 'conceit', as Shakespeare used it in sonnet cvii, was 'the mortal moon': the moon was always regarded as virginal.

W

waac: word formed from the initials of the Women's Army Auxiliary Corps in the First World War, and which became the Auxiliary Territorial Service (ATS) in the Second.

waaf: an acronym like the above: member (or members, because it was also used as a collective noun) of the Women's Auxiliary Air Force, established in 1939.

wake, the: see *Hereward the wake*.

Walkerites: followers of John Walker (1768–1833) who left the Church of England and founded a Calvinistic sect in Dublin. He was author of scholarly works, classical and mathematical.

wallflowers: like the flowers that grow modestly against the garden wall, clinging to the stonework (and not necessarily the blooms of that name), the girls who sit at the side of the dance floor without partners.

wallpaper: broadcast or recorded ('canned') music played in the background to normal activity, at home, at work or in a store, needing no particular concentration, taken for granted as is the wallpaper which surrounds us.

warming pans: provocative nickname given to the Jacobites q.v. by those who professed to believe the rumour that James Francis Edward Stuart, the 'old pretender' q.v., when a baby, was smuggled into the bedroom of Mary of Modena—second wife of James II—in a warming pan because her own child was stillborn. The old pretender himself was given the nickname of the 'warming pan baby'.

warpaint: a woman's make-up; 'dressed to kill', as ancient tribes or red Indians smeared colour on themselves before battle. See *picts*.

wars of the roses: convenient term for the thirty years of conflict between the houses of York and Lancaster for the crown of England, usually considered to have begun with the battle of St Albans, 1455, and to have ended at Bosworth, 1485, with the death of Richard III and the accession of Henry VII who married princess Elizabeth of York, thus uniting the two factions. The conflicting sides took roses as their emblems—York white, Lancaster red.

The war is continued annually—on the cricket field—with intense rivalry between the Yorkshire and Lancashire county teams, so that the term has had a new connotation ever since the county championship was instituted in 1872. Newspaper headlines for the matches between these two counties each year are invariably 'War of the Roses' or 'The Roses Match'.

Watergate: a complex of flats, offices and an hotel in Washington where the Democratic National Committee had its headquarters on the sixth floor of the office block, the word becoming synonymous with a scandal which resulted in the resignation of the president, Richard Nixon in 1974. Agents of the Committee to Re-elect the President (CREEP) were caught breaking into the Democratic headquarters with burglars' tools and bugging devices in 1972. Connections with the White House were first revealed by reporters from the *Washington Post*, and an investigation into the affair and attempts at 'cover-up' was carried out by a Senate select committee. The word, familiarised in British newspapers and books, was adopted to describe other—lesser—public scandals, with phrases such as 'Another Watergate' or 'Doing a Watergate'. See *tricky Dickie*.

water poet, the: John Taylor (1580–1653), apprenticed to a Thames waterman, and after being pressed into the navy he returned to become a waterman. He appears to have conferred the title on himself, and people accepted it as part of his eccentricity and self-advertisement. He wrote rollicking rhymes, but was no poet: he was more successful as a witty pamphleteer and writer about his travels. On one occasion he sailed in a paper boat; he walked from London to Scotland; and he travelled as far as Prague for a wager.

wavy navy, the: Royal Navy Volunteer Reserve (RNVR), because the bands denoting rank were serrated, in contrast with the straight ones of the regular service.

Wedgie: Anthony Wedgwood Benn, when he was secretary of state for industry in the Labour government of 1975, not only as a contraction of his name but because his Conservative opponents saw him as driving a wedge of complete socialism into the constitution, with his plans for nationalisation and seeming hostility towards private enterprise. A satirical note in *The Guardian*, 13 May, 1975, referred to 'the suffering, the huddled masses cringing under the lash of the wicked Wedgie'. A radio programme about the industry bill was entitled in

Radio Times: 'Thin End of the Wedge?' The *Daily Mirror*, 29 May, 1975, went even further and dubbed him 'the Minister of Fear', saying: 'Mr Benn is playing on one of the nation's deepest anxieties, the fear of unemployment.'

Wee Frees, the: members of the minority within the Free Church of Scotland who firmly refused in 1900 to join with the United Presbyterians in forming the United Free Church of Scotland; strict in religious observance, strongly Calvinistic.

weepers: (1) long side whiskers: see 'dundrearies' and 'piccadilly weepers'; (2) the darkly-dressed and doleful hired mourners at a funeral, a strange nineteenth-century custom for those who could afford these dismal gentry. The custom goes much further back, although the professional mourners had not generally been nicknamed 'weepers'. *The Connoisseur*, No. 39, 1754, reproved the ostentation of a cheese-monger's funeral, the family aping their betters: 'I was stopped by a grand procession of a hearse and three mourning-coaches drawn by six horses, accompanied with a great number of flambeaus and attendants in black.' The nickname 'weepers' was also applied in the nineteenth century to a widow's black veil and to the black bands which men wore on their hats as a token of mourning.

wellingtons: originally a high boot reaching the knee and cut away behind it, as worn by the first duke of Wellington when a soldier on campaign; latterly a rubber boot as high as the knee.

Welsh wizard, the: David Lloyd George, earl of Dwyfor (1863–1945), because of his long and distinguished political career, his oratory and persuasiveness. Although born in Manchester he was brought up in Wales and was a solicitor there, entering parliament as member for Caernarvon boroughs. Among his many offices were those of chancellor and prime minister. He was a driving force in the First World War and the peace negotiations that followed. There was another 'Welsh wizard'—Billy Meredith, who captained Manchester City football team in the cup final of 1904.

wen: see *great wen.*

wet bob: an Eton scholar who goes in for boating, contrasted with 'dry bob' q.v.

whigs: the tit-for-tat nickname given by their opponents ('tories' q.v.) to the party which argued for parliamentary power over the crown and advocated toleration for dissenters at the restoration. The court party—the tories—were nick-named after Irish outlaws, and the whigs got their abusive name from Scottish rebels and horse-thieves, 'whig' probably coming from *whigamore*. *ODEE* suggests it is a shortening of *whiggamaire*—*whig* meaning drive, *mere*, a horse. There have been other ingenious attempts at the derivation of the word, one of them being that it comprised the initials of the coven-anters' motto, 'We hope in God', and certainly it was once applied to the covenanters. Whatever the explanation, whigs and tories were lined-up against each other from the latter part of the seventeenth century, although their policies changed over the years, and whigs became dominant in the following century. Whigs lost their name to 'Liberals', but the tories kept theirs as an alternative to 'Conservatives'. Why this should be so is difficult to explain.

whip: a member of a parliamentary party chosen to ensure the attendance of his colleagues at important debates in the chamber, especially necessary when a government has a small majority and every vote is needed at a division; the word taken from the whip, the man responsible for the hounds in the hunt. 'Whip' is also used for the notice of business sent to members, the importance or urgency indicated by underlining the words—such as 'a three line whip'. Whips also arrange 'pairing' with an opposition party when members have to be absent at voting time in the house of commons.

whipping boy: a person who takes the blame; also transferred to something held responsible for misdemeanours. At one, time for example, cheap fiction and cheap newspapers were the 'whipping boy' for the lowering of public morals, then the cinema, then television. The term, or nickname, originated in the boy employed in a royal household to receive such punish-ment on behalf of the young prince who had merited it from his tutor.

whiteboys: mid-seventeenth-century land-reform groups in

Ireland which turned to violence, assembling at night with white frocks over their clothes and destroying the property of landlords, protestant clergy and tithe collectors.

white collar workers: professional and business men, clerks, etc., whose employment allows them to dress smartly in contradistinction with the manual workers. In trade union parlance, usually the clerical and administrative staff.

white elephant: some useless possession; of value, perhaps, but too expensive or a nuisance to keep, like the sacred white elephant a king of Siam was reputed to have presented to a courtier whom he wished to ruin.

white man's burden: Britain's responsibility for the empire she had founded, probably coined by Kipling. 'The average Englishman considered that his word was his bond, while his country stood for trade, justice, law and order, the sanctity of contracts, the bearing of the white man's burden, the freedom of the individual and parliamentary democracy': John Montgomery, *1900: the End of an Era*, London, Allen and Unwin, 1968.

white man's grave: west Africa, with all its diseases and climatic conditions braved by the nineteenth-century explorers, missionaries and empire-builders.

white queen, the: Mary, queen of Scots (1542–87), a passing reference to her wearing white instead of the customary British mourning on the death of her first husband, Francis II of France. This was not unusual in France. Mary Tudor (sister of Henry VIII) was also called 'the white queen' when she became widow of Louis XII. '. . . custom required a royal widow of France to lie in bed for six weeks in a darkened room, lighted only by candles, and dressed in white': Desmond Seward, *Prince of the Renaissance: the Life of Francis I*, London, Constable, 1973.

whore of Babylon, the: protestant gibe at the Roman catholic church, identifying it with 'Babylon the great mother of harlots', *Revelation* xvii, and by transference to the pope himself, as in a letter to *The Spectator*, No. 616, 1714, describing the celebrations on the crowning of George I: 'At nine o'clock in the evening we set fire to the whore of Babylon.' In the next number there is another reference to burning the pope's effigy, the crowd giving 'the old gentleman several thumps upon his triple headpiece'.

wideawake: a wittily-conceived nickname for a soft felt hat with a wide brim, because it had no 'nap'.

widow at Windsor, the: queen Victoria (1819–1901) who went into seclusion for a long time after the death of Albert, prince consort, in 1861, withdrawing from public life to Windsor castle. Rudyard Kipling, with a disrespect that shocked many people, gave her this description in a poem of that title:

> 'Ave you 'eard o' the Widow at Windsor,
> With a hairy gold crown on 'er 'ead?

William rufus: William II (c1056–1100), third son of William 'the conqueror' q.v., because of his ruddy complexion. See *Rufus* for more detail.

William the conqueror: William I (1027–87), the honorific bestowed on him after his successful invasion of England in 1066 and included here (see Introduction, p. 3) only because this mighty king is rarely identified without it. He had another nickname, 'the bastard', being the illegitimate son of Robert ('the devil'), duke of Normandy, by a tanner's daughter at Falaise named Arletta.

Winchester geese: prostitutes living in houses owned by the bishop of Winchester in the Southwark district of London. Property in this area began to be turned into brothels from the fourteenth century, and by Shakespeare's time was very familiar. 'Winchester goose!' cries the duke of Gloucester to the bishop of Winchester in *I King Henry the Sixth* (I, ii) '. . . out, scarlet hypocrite!'

Winnie: Sir Winston Churchill (1874–1965) whose long, adventurous and brilliant career as statesman and writer reached its zenith when he was the inspiring prime minister during the Second World War.

woman of the town: eighteenth-century euphemism for a prostitute, much used in the journalism of the time. Typical is a letter in *The Spectator*, No. 190, 1711, purporting to be written on behalf of 'we women of the town' by an inmate of a brothel kept by Sal, a notorious London procuress, telling her life-story; and in the same number another letter beginning: 'I am to complain to you of a set of impertinent coxcombs who visit the apartments of us women of the town, only, as they call it, to see the world.' *The Connoisseur*, No. 44, 1754, defines various classes of females, from ladies of quality to demi-reps who are liberal with their favours for the sheer fun of it and ask no payment, and to 'ladies of pleasure' who do; and on the lowest rung, 'the draggle-tailed street-walker . . . liable to be sent to Bridewell'. The higher-class *cocotte* here mentioned, whose reward was often generous—even to the extent of a title—had her nickname in the previous century, as in John Evelyn's *Diary*, 1 March, 1671: 'Thence the King walked to the Duchess of Cleveland, another lady of pleasure and curse of our nation.' See also *miss*.

women's lib: a movement for the complete emancipation of women—equal educational and job opportunities, equal pay, sexual freedom and a new philosophic outlook—which gained momentum in Britain from the nineteen-sixties, although the simmering of discontent began before that as more women went out to work and involved themselves in everyday affairs. The movement took on both a sociological and political outlook, stimulated by Simone de Beauvoir's *The Second Sex* and Germaine Greer's *The Female Enuch* (1970). On the hysterical and less-serious side there was the anti-restriction slogan, 'Throw away your bras' and the epithet for men, 'male chauvinist pigs'. The male bastion was difficult to broach: a leader in the *News-Chronicle*, 2 April, 1958, had expressed the Victorian attitude: 'Both sides should keep an eye on this peaceful revolution. Women are wonderful in countless ways —but they are not at their best as masters.' And *The Guardian*, 30 April, 1975, reported: 'Simone de Beauvoir, one of the founding mothers of women's lib, today accused women of being accomplices in their own subjugation.' See *orator Hunt, suffragettes*.

woolsack, the: seat of the lord chancellor when presiding over the house of lords, extended to refer to the office itself, because it was, indeed, a sack of wool—or originally four bound sacks, placed there in the reign of Edward III as a symbol of the wool trade's importance in England's economy. The sacks were eventually replaced by a large square cushion, covered with red cloth. Wool, and cloth made from it, were for long the country's staple manufacture and export. To assist home trade two acts decreed that all corpses must be buried in wool.

world's sweetheart, the: Mary Pickford (Gladys Mary Smith), one of the first great heroines of the silent films, a protegée of D. W. Griffith. Born 1893, she began her career as a child actress and progressed to such popularity in the cinema that the honorific 'America's sweetheart' was enlarged to that of 'the world' with such films as *Daddy Longlegs* (1919), *Pollyanna* (1920), and *Little Lord Fauntleroy* (1921). After success as actress and producer she became an accomplished businesswoman.

wrens: members of the Women's Royal Naval Service.

Wycliffites: followers of John Wycliffe (c1320–84), also called 'lollards' q.v. Wycliffe (his name is spelt in several ways in old documents) is famed for his translation of the scriptures into the vernacular and for his reforming zeal, attacking clerical abuses and certain doctrines of the church, including transubstantiation. He was a powerful preacher and writer, and while not denying the sacraments maintained that they were not essential to personal salvation. He inspired John Huss and sowed some of the seeds that later grew into protestantism.

Y

yankee: originally applied to a citizen of New England, then to one residing in the northern states generally, although the British have used the nickname without much geographical reference—in the First World War to any American soldier, 'the Yanks are here'. There are several suggested origins, and you take your pick, as there is no precise documentary evidence. One is that it was how some north American Indians pronounced 'English' or the way they heard French settlers used the word *Anglais*. Another idea—and perhaps a more likely one—is that early seventeenth-century Dutch settlers in New Amsterdam (the present city of New York) applied the nickname 'Jankin', a diminutive of Jan (John), to the English of Connecticut, and the word became corrupted to 'yankee'. British soldiers in the American War of Independence classed all their opponents as 'yankees', and in the Civil War the confederates used the word for the union (northern) soldiers. 'Yankee Doodle' was an American song popular in England.

yarborough: a hand at cards (whist or bridge) in which none is of higher value than a nine, named after the nineteenth-century earl of Yarborough who used to offer high odds (a thousand to one) against such an occurrence.

year of revolutions: 1848 has been so called, because of risings in various parts of Europe—notably France, Italy, Austria and Prussia—and industrial and political unrest in England, with a revival of the 'chartists' q.v. agitation, the duke of Wellington bringing out troops to prevent their march on parliament. The 'chartists', whose demands for radical reforms had persisted for ten years, aroused tremendous fears in London and several parts of the country, businessmen and politicians considering them revolutionaries for whom armed force was the only answer.

yellow-backs: nickname given to the cheaper romantic novels which began to be published in the eighteen-fifties, with illustrated covers and usually a yellow background. There had been a custom of re-issuing the 'three-decker' q.v. novel in one volume, and this popularisation was taken a step further with the publication at one or two shillings of a special edition of fiction aimed primarily at railway travellers, W. H. Smith having established bookstalls on many of the stations. These 'yellow backs', once so familiar, are now collectors' pieces.

yellow press, the: sensational journalism; newspapers bidding for readers' attention with 'scare stories' and 'revelations' of public and private scandal; an American term from 1895 and adopted in Britain around the turn of the century as one of abuse against the cheaper newspapers with brighter make-up, eye-attracting headlines, brash reporting and pictures. The description was coined in New York when William Randolph Hearst bought the *Journal* and entered into remorseless competition with Joseph Pulitzer's *World*. Hearst obtained the services of a cartoonist who had been contributing a popular comic picture series called 'The Yellow Kid' to the *Sunday World*, but another artist took his place and continued the series for Pulitzer. So that there were two 'Yellow Kids' competing for attention, and along with this rivalry went experiments in presentation, such as banner headlines, and 'comic' strips and illustrations, and behind-the-scenes reports, all of which became known as 'yellow journalism'.

yorker: a high-swinging ball at cricket, delivered by the bowler as directly at the bat without bouncing as possible, presumably a technique attributed originally to the Yorkshire side.

young pretender, the: Charles Edward (Louis Philip Casimir) Stuart (1720–88), also called the 'young chevalier', elder son of James, the 'old pretender' q.v. for whose claim to the English throne he initiated the uprising in 1745. Charles Edward was a brave and handsome young man, and his ill-fated advance from Scotland as far as Derby, his retreat and escape to France, made him a romantic figure. (See the '*forty-five*'). He was a hero to the Highlanders—'bonnie prince Charlie'—and also to the people of Paris—for a time. He became an embarrassment to the French government, wandered through Europe in search of help for a hopeless cause, lapsed into drunkenness and debauchery.

young Roscius, the: see *Roscius*.

Z

zany: an idiot, a preposterous fool, also a mimic because it was originally the theatrical name for a buffoon who mimicked the clown in Italian comedy (*commedia dell' arte*), the diminutive of the Italian Giovanni (John), and it was transferred as a nickname for anyone considered to be foolish or ridiculous. It was familiar as such in Shakespeare's day, because Berowne uses it in *Love's Labour's Lost* (V, ii): 'Some carry-tale, some please-man, some slight zany.' (Surely, too, this was in some ways Shakespeare's zaniest comedy!) It is interesting to note that this English adoption of the diminutive of Giovanni has been carried forward to our own Johnny for John, in such an expression as 'He's a silly Johnny'. Johnny has been used as a nickname in several ways, including that for a man-about-town: cf. the Edwardian 'stage door Johnny', the fop waiting for a favourite actress to come out. Zany lingered in the vocabulary but was almost forgotten by the nineteenth century; and then the Americans retrieved it—as with so many old English words—and refurbished it. A favourite description of the Marx brothers' films was 'zany comedy': the word has come to mean outrageous foolery.

zebra crossing: the safety path for pedestrians between opposite pavements on a road, so named because it is painted in stripes, black and white. There are traffic regulations appertaining to such crossings. See *Belisha beacon*.

Zinoviev letter, the: a sensational political 'scare' in 1924 when a letter purporting to be signed by Grigory E. Zinoviev, president of the Third International, was published just before a general election. The letter, which turned out to be a forgery, called on the British Communist party to carry out subversive activities. This 'red letter scare' undoubtedly helped the Conservatives to win the election. The Russians denied its authenticity.

Index

(of proper names and of words as subjects, or with significant relevance in the entries)